HOMECOMING
100th Anniversary
1923 — 2023

A History of Its First 100 Years

Conniston Road
(1923-1949)

North Olive Avenue
(1949-1965)

36th Street
(1965-1998)

Leo Lane
(1998-Present)

Palm Beach Lakes
CHURCH OF CHRIST

PALM BEACH LAKES CHURCH OF CHRIST:
A History of Its First 100 Years

Copyright © 2023 by   Palm Beach Lakes church of Christ
                         4067 Leo Lane
                         Palm Beach Gardens, FL 33410

All rights reserved. No part of this book may be reproduced in any form without written permission from the author.

ISBN: 9798396584488

— Introduction —

Nearly 2,000 years ago, Jesus Christ walked this earth and made His wonderful promise, "On this rock I will build My church, and the gates of Hades shall not prevail against it" (Matt. 16:18). That church, which God promised would "never be destroyed" and would "stand forever" (Dan. 2:44), found its way to the West Palm Beach, Florida area over 100 years ago. Then, in 1923, inside sister Lena B. Eades' home, a congregation of the Lord's church had its small beginnings. For almost 50 years, the congregation was known as the "Central church of Christ," but on July 13, 1969, it officially became the "Palm Beach Lakes church of Christ," taking the name of the local community in which it was found at the time.

It has been said by numerous people over the years, *"Palm Beach Lakes is a special place."* No doubt, every congregation of the Lord's people around the world must feel that way about their home congregation. The Lord's church truly is special! The Divine love that planned for it, the price that was paid for it and the bond that the body of Christ has with its Head makes His church (and being part of His church) an immeasurable blessing. Still, there seem to be some qualities that have long characterized the Palm Beach Lakes congregation that make those who have been part of it feel a tight bond with each other.

What are those unique qualities? In many ways, it may be difficult to identify them or enumerate them. What makes Palm Beach Lakes what it is? Perhaps it is the strong leadership it has had, or its deep devotion to preaching sound doctrine, or its ongoing focus on seeking lost souls, or its fervent love for one another, or its perpetual dream of being together in heaven. What makes Palm Beach Lakes "Palm Beach Lakes"? Simply stated: It's the people! The church is not a building—we know that. The church is the people. And for 100 years, Palm Beach Lakes has been made up of some of the most special people on earth, who have formed some very special bonds.

This book contains a brief history and reproduction of the records that June Haines Pack has kept over the years. It is not a perfect or complete record of all things or all people who have been part of Palm Beach Lakes. It is a human production after all. But, perhaps you will find enjoyment in reading about the beginning of this congregation and some of the various people, events and milestones that have made Palm Beach Lakes what it is today.

Thank you to June Haines Pack for her diligent record keeping for the last 50 years, and to Cindy Nelson for compiling, converting and editing all of the information. We apologize for any names that are misspelled or for other errors in the records. The file and text conversion is about 98% accurate, but we are not certain that we found all of the mistakes in our proofing process.

— Table of Contents —

Items of Interest Before Log Began in 1973 4

1923-1973 6

1973-1979 8

1980-1989 32

1990-1999 78

2000-2009 124

2010-2019 172

2020-2023 214

Mission Sunday & Supported Works 236

List of Gospel Meetings 240

List of Ladies' Days 242

List of Lectureships 244

List of Men Who Have Served As Elders 247

List of Men Who Have Served As Deacons 248

List of Men Who Have Served As Preachers 250

List of Secretaries / Office Staff 252

— Items of Interest Before Log Began in 1973 —

Dec. 14, 1958	First Lake Park property bought. Final payment.
Mar. 15, 1959	Meeting with Hugh Piper (WPB), Max Johnson (Andrews Ave.), Dan Gilbert (Ft. Myers), J. Leo Snow (Miami), Richard Blackman (Pompano), and George Darling (Ft. Pierce) through March 21
June 28, 1959	Hugh Piper left after five years here.
June 1, 1960	W. Ray Duncan came to serve as a preacher.
Sep. 25, 1960	Attendance check began
Oct. 6, 1960	First Lake Park property sold and the second was bought
Mar. 26, 1961	First church directories were printed.
July 22, 1961	First TV program - "Know Your Bible" with W. Ray Duncan
Oct. 1, 1961	Began having two morning services until August 25, 1963
Feb. 4, 1962	Membership: 200
Feb. 16, 1962	Decision made to sell all properties and build on 36th Street
July 1, 1962	Bert Brown was here as second preacher until January 1, 1963.
June 1, 1963	Purchase of 36th Street property was complete.
June 5, 1963	Second class mailing permit was obtained to mail bulletins.
Sep. 15, 1963	Six-month training class taught by brother Duncan
Dec. 1, 1963	Membership: 243
Apr. 12, 1964	Elders ordained: Jean McMasters, Hayward Milton, Don Spurlock and Alvin Witt. Up until this time, decisions were made in men's business meetings with B.F. Burleson, Red Johnson, Harvey Fort and Jimmy Carter serving as trustees.
June 2, 1964	Church incorporated
Nov. 14, 1964	Benson & Bales two-day debate on Communism
Oct. 1964	Northside began with a small group who were not satisfied with the decision to build on 36th Street. They met in a store on Park Avenue.
Dec. 6, 1964	Ground breaking for new building on 36th Street
Dec. 30, 1964	New Year's Eve parties began
Jan. 4, 1965	Marcus Crews sent as missionary to Australia until January 7, 1968.
July 18, 1965	Grand opening of new building on 36th Street (with Bill Hatcher as speaker)
July 18, 1965	Membership: 256

— Items of Interest Before Log Began in 1973 —

Apr. 11, 1966	Ten-day debate between Ray Duncan and E.L. Johnson (Baptist) in White City
Jan. 1, 1967	Membership: 300
Jan. 22, 1967	Wayne Speer came as assistant preacher for about one year.
Mar. 1967	TV program "Know Your Bible" ended after six years
Apr. 24, 1967	Ann Haines became secretary until February 11, 1968.
Aug. 6, 1967	Bus trip to Harding for a one-week lectureship
Sep. 1967	Marshall Keeble held a meeting for the 18th Street congregation in our building.
May 19, 1968	Jean McMasters resigned as elder
Aug. 4, 1968	W. Ray Duncan resigned as preacher
Dec. 20, 1968	Bill Hatcher accepted work here and arrived December 29, 1968.
Jan. 12, 1969	Pictures of members placed in foyer
Jan. 30, 1969	Bill Hatcher went to India until April 5, 1969.
July 13, 1969	Name of the church changed to Palm Beach Lakes church of Christ
Aug. 5, 1969	Gerald Pace sent as missionary to Australia. He died in 1973.
Jan. 18, 1970	John Weisenburger resigned as treasurer after seven years. Bill Ingram, Sr. replaced him and served for many years.
Feb. 4, 1970	New TV program with Bill Hatcher began
Feb. 12, 1970	First "Circles of Truth" classes with Bill Hatcher began
Feb. 15, 1970	Alvin Witt resigned as elder due to poor health
1971	Dane Waggoner left for Puerto Rico
Aug. 1, 1972	Larry Grizzell came to work as second preacher and left in November 1973.
June 1, 1973	Bill & Mary Sproule began work as church custodians.

— 1923 to 1973 —

This congregation had its beginning in 1923, in the home of sister Lena B. Eades on Okeechobee Road. Two years later, it had grown sufficiently so that with a gift of land from a brother Chamberlain, a meetinghouse was erected on Conniston Road. The first official meeting in the new building was held September 20, 1925. Two of our members who worshipped in sister Eades home were Frank Johnson and L.A. Reeder.

The first regular preacher at Conniston Road was Henry Clay Geer, 1925-1928; followed by Warren Colson, 1928-1931; Alfred Traylor, 1931-1932; Ethany Shoulders, 1932-1935; Russell King, 1935-1939, 1942-1945; M. Cecil Perryman, 1939-1942; Bill Floyd, 1945-1948; Iverson L. Boles, 1948-1950.

As the congregation grew, there was a need for larger facilities. A gift of land from sister Bertie Walden and a $10,000 donation from sister Eades made possible the erection of a new building and home for the preacher at 811 North Olive Avenue. The first worship services were held in the building in June 1949, while I.L. Boles was the minister. Brother Boles was followed by John Renshaw, 1950-1954; Hugh Piper, 1955-1959; Eugene Pitts, 1959; W.E. Black, Bert Brown, and W. Ray Duncan, 1960-1968.

The organization of the church was made complete on April 12, 1964, with the ordaining of four elders: Jean McMasters, Hayward Milton, Don Spurlock, and Alvin Witt. On February 7, 1965, four men were selected to serve as deacons: Johnny Davis, Bob Haines, Jerry Hopkins, and Paul Jordan.

In June 1963, five acres were purchased on 36th Street, and on December 6, 1964, ground was broken and a new and modern church plant, complete with classrooms, was begun. The total cost of construction was $250,000, plus $40,000 for the land. The formal opening was on July 18, 1965, with a membership of 256. W. Ray Duncan served the congregation at this time, and Wayne Speer worked with him for about one year as educational director. William C. (Bill) Hatcher began his work with us on December 29, 1968 and still served the congregation as this was written in 1973, along with Larry Grizzell who joined him in this work on August 6, 1972.

After entering our new building, additional deacons were selected and some changes made in the eldership. Paul Jordan had moved to Ft. Lauderdale in 1965. On October 2, 1966, seven additional deacons were selected: Pete Brown, Lowell Flowers, Bill Ingram, Charles Kulp, Tom Mitchell, Bill Powell and Doug Renahan. Jean McMasters had resigned as elder in May 1968, and Alvin Witt, because of poor health, in March 1970. Harold Keathley was ordained as an elder on August 30, 1970; Jerry Hopkins on October 17, 1971; and Fred Faulkner on September 17, 1972. Marty Wingo was selected as deacon in December 1970. Charles Kulp moved away in April 1971, and Lowell Flowers resigned on September 17, 1972, leaving us with eight dea-

— 1923 to 1973 —

cons and five elders. As of December 31, 1972, the membership consisted of 163 families and 312 members.

Elders
Fred Faulkner
Jerry Hopkins
Harold Keathley
Hayward Milton
Don Spurlock

Evangelists
William C. Hatcher
Larry Grizzell

Missionaries
Gerald Pace (Australia)
Jack Fogerty (Puerto Rico)
Dane Waggoner (Puerto Rico)
George O'Briant (Canada)

Deacons
Pete Brown
Johnny Davis
Bob Haines
Bill Ingram, Sr.
Tom Mitchell
Bill Powell
Doug Renahan
Marty Wingo

— 1973 —

The year 1973 proved to be a very full one for the members of the church at Palm Beach Lakes. Our meeting scheduled for January with Willard Collins was cancelled due to his illness. In February, a new visitation program was started, with different families meeting on Monday nights for eight-week periods, calling on absentee members and visitors. In April, our Zone system was revised from seven zones to four.

Two of our elders, Harold Keathley and Don Spurlock, journeyed to Tasmania in June to get a first-hand report on the work there.

During the first six months of the year, sixty-two of our members completed the course "Adventures in Christian Living" by Ron Willingham taught by Larry Grizzell. Also many of our members became involved in a daily Bible reading program that would enable one to read the entire Bible in a year.

Five additional deacons were selected on June 17: Gerald Bobo, Jesse Ford, Dewayne Lanham, Gary Morton and Russell Waggoner. One of our deacons, Marty Wingo, moved to Pennsylvania in July.

Brother Hatcher moved his office into his home on July 1, where he began to put some of his material into book form.

Judy Witt became church secretary on August 13, replacing Frankie Mitchell, who had served for four years.

Our hearts were saddened in September by the passing of two faithful laborers in Tasmania. Joe Salmon died as a result of an automobile accident, and Gerald Pace died from cancer.

A Golden Years Banquet was held on September 22 in honor of our older members and enjoyed by many.

A door-knocking campaign was conducted during September with 72 members visiting 2,200 homes in the area during a five-week period.

Johnny Ramsey from Garland, Texas conducted our fall meeting on October 7-12 with eight responses.

Larry Grizzell submitted his resignation in November, and on December 15, he moved to Lincoln Park, Michigan to work with the church there.

During this year, there were twenty-two baptisms and twenty-five identified with this congregation. Twenty of our members moved away, leaving us with a membership of 173 families and 340 members.

— 1973 —

Elders
Fred Faulkner
Jerry Hopkins
Harold Keathley
Hayward Milton
Don Spurlock

Evangelists
William C. Hatcher

Missionaries
Ray Winn (Tasmania)
Jack Fogerty (Puerto Rico)
Dan Waggoner (Puerto Rico)
George O'Briant (Canada)

Deacons
Gerald Bobo
Pete Brown
Johnny Davis
Jesse Ford
Bob Haines
Bill Ingram, Sr.
Dewayne Lanham
Tom Mitchell
Gary Morton
Bill Powell
Doug Renahan
Russell Waggoner

— 1974 —

Our spring meeting was held on January 20-27 with Cleon Lyles from Little Rock, Arkansas.

In February, several ten-week classes were begun. Bill Hatcher taught a class on Jehovah's Witnesses, Fred Faulkner taught the Jr. High boys, and Mona Faulkner taught the Jr. High girls. These classes were on Sunday evenings at 6:00 p.m. just before regular Sunday evening services. At the same time, Dewayne Lanham began a class for those who wanted to learn new songs in our songbook and how to sing the old ones better. This continued all year.

The Ray Winn family was finally able to leave for Tasmania on March 12 to begin their work there.

On April 12-13, thirty of our young people attended the annual Harding Youth Forum in Searcy, Arkansas.

A Youth Rally was held here on May 25-26 with services all day Saturday and both services Sunday with Gary Martin from Searcy, Arkansas.

Dane Waggoner returned from Puerto Rico in July and moved to Kentucky to begin a new work there.

Dean & Fran Reynolds joined us on August 1 to work primarily with the visitation program. Maxie Boren conducted our fall meeting on September 22-27. It was one of the best attended meetings by our own members that we ever had. There were 9 baptisms and one restoration.

Kerry & Tommie Cain came to work with us on November 1, after spending seven years in New Zealand. They lived in the home on Dory Road in North Palm Beach, owned by Palm Beach Lakes.

The Golden Years Banquet to honor our older members was on November 9.

The year was closed out with our annual New Year's party, consisting of congregational talent and a devotional.

During the year, there were thirty-three baptisms and forty-three identified with us. Forty moved away and three died. This leaves us with a membership of 177 families and 356 members.

— 1974 —

Elders
Fred Faulkner
Jerry Hopkins
Harold Keathley
Hayward Milton
Don Spurlock

Evangelists
William C. Hatcher
Kerry Cain

Missionaries
Ray Winn (Tasmania)
Jack Fogerty (Puerto Rico)
Dan Waggoner (Puerto Rico)
George O'Briant (Canada)

Deacons
Gerald Bobo
Pete Brown
Johnny Davis
Jesse Ford
Bob Haines
Bill Ingram, Sr.
Dewayne Lanham
Tom Mitchell
Gary Morton
Bill Powell
Doug Renahan
Russell Waggoner

— 1975 —

June Haines began working as full-time secretary on January 1.

This year began with a Seminar on the Christian home on January 3-5, conducted by Paul Faulkner of Abilene, Texas.

Charles Salmon visited us on January 12 from Tasmania, Australia, and gave us a report on the work being done there.

Jesse Ford was ordained an elder, and Doug Carmack and Tom Holaday were appointed deacons on March 30.

Twenty-nine of our teens again journeyed to Searcy, Arkansas, to attend the annual Youth Forum at Harding College on March 27-31.

A special contribution was planned for March 30 to make up the deficit in the budget and $8,241 was given.

Otis Gatewood conducted our spring meeting on April 13-17.

In May, we began using the series of tracts by Johnny Ramsey on the books of the Bible, handing out a different one each Sunday.

Fred Faulkner resigned as elder on June 1.

Ray & Marilyn Winn were blessed by the birth of a baby daughter, Denita Ann, on July 23 in Tasmania, Australia.

Bill Hatcher was in South Africa for two-and-a-half months, from August 1 to October 10, for a series of meetings and lectureships and some teaching in the schools of preaching there.

A work program was organized in August to paint the entire building, including the new classroom complex, with a different deacon or elder in charge each Saturday for several months. This saved the congregation a considerable amount of money.

Jim Waldron from Australia held a three-day meeting for us on August 10-12.

A training program for new converts began in the fall with different teachers for thirteen sessions.

We began using the new classrooms on October 5. At this time a count of daily Bible readers began each week.

Ira Rice was our guest speaker on October 26, delivering a message on liberalism in the church.

Ira North was vacationing in the area on November 16 and spoke to us at the evening worship service.

The annual Golden Years Banquet was on December 6.

— 1975 —

Elders
Jesse Ford
Jerry Hopkins
Harold Keathley
Hayward Milton
Don Spurlock

Deacons
Gerald Bobo
Pete Brown
Doug Carmack
Johnny Davis
Bob Haines
Bill Ingram, Sr.
Tom Holaday
Dewayne Lanham
Tom Mitchell
Gary Morton
Bill Powell
Doug Renahan
Russell Waggoner

Evangelists
William C. Hatcher
Kerry Cain
Dean Reynolds

College
Walter Arthur, Jr.
Dennis Faulkner
Peggy Gregory
Michael Hatcher
Debi Ingram
Bill Ingram, Jr.
Elaine Knowles
Bobby Knowles
Ron McQuinn
Karen Terrana
Milton Wickles
Bobby Haines

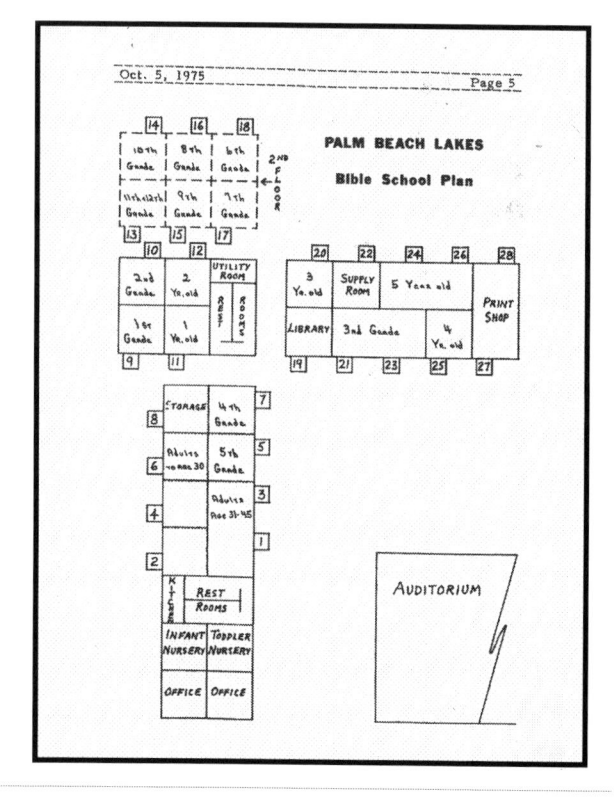

— 1975 —

Baptized (34)
Feb. 17 Everett Hatfield
Mar. 30 Janna Hopkins
Mar. 30 Mrs. Ralph Cook
Mar. 31 Alex Ray
Apr. 07 Amy Ray
Apr. 10 Alan Oldham
Apr. 10 Chip Carmack
Apr. 19 Alice Anderson
Apr. 20 Joel Palmer
Apr. 20 Craig Lanham
Apr. 20 Beth Bobo
Apr. 20 Chris Keathley
Apr. 29 Beverly Goodwill
May 11 Sabrina Renahan
May 15 Jackie Phillips
May 25 Don Deel
June 01 Derek & Darnell Wood
June 08 Nancy Fields
June 25 Donna Lynn Smith
Aug. 01 Joey Hanna
Aug. 01 Annette Cannon
Aug. 01 Lisa Terry
Aug. 13 Anita Riddle
Sep. 10 Michelle Mayer
Sep. 14 Albert Pradetto
Sep. 17 Linda Martin
Oct. 12 Mary Land
Oct. 28 Jeff Riddle
Oct. 28 Debbie Jaress
Nov. 02 Luci Pribble
Nov. 09 Jim Hardee
Dec. 10 Connie Griffin
Dec. 14 Victor Banuelos

Identified (20)
Jan. 12 John & Margie Weisanen
Jan. 12 Alvie O. & Georgia Davis
Feb. 02 Cathy Newberry
Feb. 23 Ron & Nancy Farley
Mar. 09 Sidney Hart
Mar. 19 Ann Hart
Apr. 27 Emma Graham
June 22 Milton Wickles
July 20 Cathy Hart
Aug. 03 Bill & Carol Anstis
Sep. 17 Sue Terry
Oct. 05 Woolen family
Nov. 16 Jim Howard

Restored (1)
Sep. 07 Joy Judd

Total Additions: 55

— 1975 —

Died (1)

Jan. 16   Frank Johnson

Moved Away (15)

Feb.	Tim Howard
May	Joel Palmer
May	Hank & Mary Flowers
May	Lucy Bond
May	Mrs. Ralph Cook
Aug.	Jim & Judy Howell
Aug.	Flossie Madden
Sep.	Kim Yeager
Sep.	Bob & Barbara Johnson
Nov.	Debbie Jaress
Dec.	Betty Lail
Dec.	Melanie Mitchell

Moved Membership (7)

Feb.	Carl Howard family (4)
Nov.	Jerry Swan
Dec.	Albert Pradetto
Dec.	Sue Terry

Total Losses: 33   **186 Families; 379 Members**

— 1976 —

The 6:00 p.m. Sunday singing practice resumed on January 11. Dewayne Lanham conducted a class at the same time for young men who wanted to learn how to lead singing.

Jerry Hogg from Benoni, South Africa spoke on January 18.

Our spring meeting was conducted on February 22-27 with brother Elmer Morgan of Dallas, Texas as the speaker. There were three requesting prayers and one baptism.

A group of our young people attended the annual Youth Forum at Harding College in Searcy, Arkansas on April 15-19. Several also attended the Junior/Senior Banquet in Fort Lauderdale in May.

On May 30, the church assumed the sponsorship of Buddy and Jeannie Lawrenson to go to South Africa the next year.

Brother Paul Hunton, associated with the Christian Counseling Clinic in Orlando, was our guest speaker on June 20.

Don Latham, who has spent five years in Trinidad, spoke on June 28.

One of our deacons, Gary Morton, moved away on August 29.

We had two guest speakers in September: Arlin Chapman, of the Florida School of Preaching in Lakeland, on the 12th, and Athens Clay Pullias, President of David Lipscomb College in Nashville, Tennessee, on the 19th.

Joe Holland agreed to work with the youth group in September after Gary and Shirley Morton moved to Arkansas.

The Golden Years Banquet was held on October 16.

Dan Jenkins, who preaches for the Shades Mountain congregation in Birmingham, Alabama, spoke to us on October 20-21 and presented new Bible class material which will be used here beginning the first of the year.

New classes were begun for the young people in November at 6:00 p.m. on Sunday.

On Sunday, November 14, Johnny Davis and Joe Holland were ordained as elders of this congregation.

Many of our young people attended a two-day Youth Rally at Stuart on December 10-11. They were so impressed with the Bible Bowl, this congregation decided to build a Bible Bowl electronic quiz machine of its own.

George Walden, Director of Admissions and Financial Aid for David Lipscomb College, spoke to our teens and interested parents on Wednesday, December 15.

One of our deacons, Bob Haines, passed away on December 30.

— 1976 —

Elders
Johnny Davis
Jesse Ford
Joe Holland
Jerry Hopkins
Harold Keathley
Don Spurlock
Hayward Milton

Deacons
Gerald Bobo
Pete Brown
Doug Carmack
Tom Holaday
Bill Ingram, Sr.
Dewayne Lanham
Tom Mitchell
Bill Powell
Doug Renahan
Russell Waggoner

Evangelists
William C. Hatcher
Kerry Cain
Dean Reynolds

Missionaries
Ray Winn (Tasmania, Australia)

Preacher Training School
Buddy Lawrenson
Jack W. Brown
Rick Brown

College
Walter Arthur, Jr.
Dennis Faulkner
Peggy Gregory
Bill Ingram, Jr.
Kym Ingram
Phil Keathley
Bobby Knowles
Terri Mitchell

— 1976 —

Baptized (13)
Jan. 18 Wes Holland
Jan. 21 Trent Hanna
Feb. 29 Jeff Burgess
Mar. 14 Melodie Mott Des Ormeaux
Apr. 07 George Sims
Apr. 11 Tina Bergeron
Apr. 11 Joy Keathley
Apr. 25 Jeff Sims
May 02 Jimmie Sue Sims
May 03 Melanie Prince
May 09 Jim Sims
June 27 Keith Price
Aug. 01 Cynthia LoBello

Restored (5)
Mar. 31 Terry Keathley
Apr. 11 Nick Hanna
Nov. 14 Clayton & Barbara Douglas
Nov. 21 Bobby Haines

Identified (24)
Jan. 07 Austen & Phyllis Moore
Mar. 03 Linda Joiner
Apr. 04 Bill & Helen Hamilton
May 16 Debbie Kay Seay
June 20 Jim Van Sleet family (3)
June 27 Bob & Connie Brooks
July 11 Victor Banuelos
Aug. 01 May Evans
Sep. 19 Dorothy & Greg Kimble
Sep. 19 Margaret Drown
Sep. 26 Victor & Mary Jane Rohrer
Oct. 10 Hugh & Linda Horrocks
Nov. 28 Richard & Sue Johnson
Dec. 19 Joe & Lois Alcock

Total Additions: 42

— 1976 —

Died (4)
Jul.26   Joe Pruss
Oct. 26   Stanley Briggs
Nov. 01   Ed Anstis
Dec. 30   Bob Haines

Moved Away (36)
Feb. 01   Sidney Hart family (3)
Feb. 15   Victor Banuelos
Mar. 01   Wayne & Jan Whitcher
Mar. 28   Ron & Nancy Farley
Apr. 01   Chuck Woolen family (4)
May 09   Marie Fox
June 01   Karen Terrana
June 01   Milton Wickles
June 29   Dick & Diane Burnette
July 02   Debi Ingram
July 02   Ron McQuinn
July 11   Rita, Leesa & Robin Sovine
Aug. 01   Greg & Michelle Morris
Aug. 22   Cindy Powell
Aug. 22   Jim Howard
Aug. 29   Jack Riddle family (4)
Aug. 29   Gary Morton family (4)
Sep. 08   Linda Joiner
Sep. 25   Lisa Smedley

Moved Membership (8)
Feb. 01   Jerry Higgins (5)
Mar. 07   Phyllis Smallridge
Dec. 05   Norman & Marie Smedley

Total Losses: 62   **188 Families; 370 Members**

- 19 -

— 1977 —

E. R. Brannan, President of Alabama Christian College, was our guest speaker on January 16.

Wade & Margie Bates left on January 23 for Lubbock, Texas to enroll at the Sunset School of Preaching.

Our spring meeting was conducted by Wyatt Sawyer from Ft. Worth, Texas, on January 30-February 3.

Greeters were appointed to be at the doors following worship services on Sundays beginning in February. Two adult couples and two teenage couples are to be used each week.

Buddy & Jeannie Lawrenson visited us for a short time in March before leaving for South Africa. They arrived in Cape Town on March 31.

Shirley Curry, of Brownsville, Tennessee, spoke to the women concerning the ERA legislation on March 17.

Work parties were conducted at the building each Saturday for six weeks beginning in April.

Jesse Ford resigned as an elder of this congregation in June.

Dwight Smith, from Tabernacle, New Jersey, was our guest speaker on August 7 and delivered a lesson on "Total Commitment."

The "Dial-A-Visit" program began by Dean Reynolds in August.

One of our deacons, Doug Renahan, moved away on August 24.

The Ladies' Bible Class on Wednesday mornings was taught by Mona Faulkner beginning in September.

Special training classes for a limited number of boys began in September by Kerry Cain. This class met at 6:00 p.m. on Sunday evenings.

New study material with the use of cards began in October. This was for all classes, except for the adults taught by Bill Hatcher and Joe Holland.

A new converts class taught by Kerry Cain on Wednesday evenings started in October.

Jerry Dyer, who had worked in Australia for several years, spoke to us concerning that work on October 30.

The annual Golden Age Banquet was held December 17.

— 1977 —

Elders
Johnny Davis
Joe Holland
Jerry Hopkins
Harold Keathley
Hayward Milton
Don Spurlock

Deacons
Gerald Bobo
Pete Brown
Doug Carmack
Tom Holaday
Bill Ingram, Sr.
Dewayne Lanham
Bill Powell
Russell Waggoner

Evangelists
William C. Hatcher
Kerry Cain
Dean Reynolds

Missionaries
Ray Winn (Tasmania)
Buddy Lawrenson (South Africa)

Preacher Training School
Wade Bates

College
Rickie Bonk
Mark Carpenter
Janet Fealy
Bill Ingram, Jr.
Phil Keathley
Jim Leslie
Terri Mitchell
Melva Naranjo
Carol Oler
Denise Ouellette
Alex Ray
Joyce Resnick

— 1977 —

Baptized (20)

Jan. 05	Chuck Reeves
Jan. 23	Kristy Terrana
Feb. 04	Ann Strother
Feb. 27	Rickie Bonk
Feb. 27	Mary Ramberg
Mar. 01	Bob Judd
Apr. 17	John Harvey
May 24	William & Ruth Jackson
May 29	Debbie Smith
July 03	Lester Young
July 09	Kathy Dean
July 13	Lisa Martin
Aug. 21	Monica Parker
Sep. 04	Linda Bowles
Sep. 11	Paul Kimble
Sep. 25	David Parker
Oct. 16	Melissa Beth Stanley
Nov. 13	Andrea & Andrew Parker

Restored (10)

Jan. 23	Pete Johnson
Jan. 23	Rita Sovine
Feb. 06	Charles & Carol Massey
Feb. 09	Ronald Henderson
Feb. 20	Tony & Doris Primicerio
May 01	Vera Cooper
May 15	Rick Taylor
Oct. 23	John Barber

Identified (37)

Jan. 02	Marilyn Dixon
Jan. 02	Teri Hahn
Jan. 09	Joe & Lois Alcock
Jan. 30	Al & Patti Crandall
Apr. 03	Flossie Harris
Apr. 20	Linda & Vicki Blass
May 22	Jim Wineinger
May 25	Wineinger family (4)
June 12	John Farrar
June 19	Janet Fealy
June 19	Joyce Resnick
June 19	Denise Ouellette
June 19	Bill Donaldson
June 19	Lee Wineinger
July 10	Allan Duguid
July 13	Reene Vaughn
July 17	Clint McKee
Aug. 28	Melva Naranjo
Aug. 28	Nancy Hardy family (4)
Sep. 11	Barbara & Debbie Jaress
Oct. 2	Susan Myers
Oct. 16	Patrick LaConte
Oct. 26	Carl & Madalyn Mack
Nov. 27	Wade & Constance Coney
Dec. 18	Virginia Warner

Total Additions: 67

— 1977 —

Died (2)
June 6   Ellis Carel
June 9   Alice Anderson

Moved Away (29)
Jan.   Peggy Gregory
Jan. 16   Mae Evans
Jan. 23   Wade & Margie Bates
Apr. 04   Cecil Sowards
May 08   Janet Fields Homan
June 05   Clayton & Barbara Douglas
June 18   Diana Pribble Bonner
June 18   Cheryl Tatar
July 08   Rick Taylor
July 31   Lester Young
Aug. 24   Renahan family (5)
Aug. 27   Dennis Faulkner
Aug. 27   Kristy Terrana Taylor
Sep. 05   Mary Carel
Sep. 18   Allan Duguid
Sep. 24   Diana Arthur
Oct. 01   Ralph Oler (AF)
Oct. 12   Marvin Freeman
Oct. 12   Flossie Harris
Oct. 23   LaRee Lumpkin
Dec. 01   Bobby & Melody Haines
Dec. 01   Reene Vaughn

Moved Membership (6)
Jan. 07   Margaret Drown
Oct. 02   Marlene Sovine
Oct. 02   Stan & Shirley Skinner
Oct. 30   Jim Wineinger
Dec. 04   Cathy Newberry

Total Losses: 54   190 Families; 366 Members

— 1978 —

Our Involvement Program began on January 8. This is an endeavor to get every member involved in the work of the congregation. Area meetings are each Sunday evening following services where assignments are made.

Our spring meeting was conducted by Maxie Boren from Corsicana, Texas on February 5-9.

J. Thomas Esmon, from Mobile, Alabama, was our guest speaker on March 12. He is associated with the Restoration Leadership Ministry in Mobile.

A New Christians' Class taught by Kerry Cain began on March 29.

Paul Hunton, from the Christian Counseling Clinic in Orlando, was our guest speaker on March 26.

Ray Winn and family returned from Australia in April and was our guest speaker on May 28.

Our new baby curriculum began in May.

The Junior/Senior Banquet was held on June 9 in Ft. Lauderdale.

Thirteen couples from this congregation attended the Marriage Enrichment Seminar in Hialeah on June 23-24 conducted by Carl Brecheen and Paul Faulkner from Abilene, Texas.

A new ladies class began in October, "The Challenge of Being A Wife," taught by Rita Lanham on Wednesday evenings.

Ed Wharton, from Lubbock, Texas, held our fall meeting on October 1-5. There were eight responses during the meeting with others following later.

Several ladies from this congregation attended the ladies encampment in Boca Raton on November 3-4.

Many of our young people attended the Youth Rally in Stuart on November 17-18.

The annual Golden Age Banquet honoring our senior members was held December 16.

Four of our elders were in Dallas, Texas to attend Wade Bates' graduation from the Preston Road School of Preaching in December.

December 31 marked ten years that Bill Hatcher has been associated with this congregation.

— 1978 —

Elders
Johnny Davis
Joe Holland
Jerry Hopkins
Harold Keathley
Hayward Milton
Don Spurlock

Deacons
Gerald Bobo
Pete Brown
Doug Carmack
Tom Holaday
Bill Ingram, Sr.
Dewayne Lanham
Tom Mitchell
Bill Powell
Russell Waggoner

Evangelists
William C. Hatcher
Kerry Cain
Dean Reynolds

Missionaries
Buddy Lawrenson (South Africa)

College
Donna Beaty
Ricky Bonk
Loni Brown
Woody & Cyndi Guin
Kerry & Linda Keathley
Kevin Keathley
Jim Leslie
Teresa Mitchell
Melva Naranjo
Denise Ouellette
Alex Ray

— 1978 —

Baptized (25)

Jan. 01	John Little
Jan. 09	Woody Guin
Feb. 08	Holly Hinlicky
Feb. 08	Grace Vega
Feb. 12	Ken & Carol Lynne Hirsh
Feb. 19	Tim Pannell
Feb. 19	John Dallas
Feb. 19	Don & Debbie Fish
Mar. 12	Jim Harris
Apr. 09	Golden Beane
June 18	Lynn Groff
July 08	Tammy Mauney
July 09	Linda Sovis
July 30	Kim Spurlock
Aug. 09	Willie Irvin
Aug. 11	Art Thayres
Sep. 14	Karen Swartz
Oct. 05	Susan Groff
Oct. 05	Connie Sproule
Oct. 07	Toni Banuelos
Oct. 08	James Weil
Nov. 08	Marie Irvin
Dec. 10	Judy Portz

Identified (37)

Jan. 15	Dianne Frye
Jan. 29	Joan Holloway
Feb. 05	Jodie Cunningham
Feb. 05	Ron & Elizabeth Brackett
Mar. 05	Martha Myers
Mar. 05	Sherrie Anderson
Mar. 19	Charles White
Apr. 16	Allen & Connie Gunn
July 05	Claudia Reese
July 30	Roger & Sandy Shell
Aug. 13	Donna Beaty
Aug. 13	Rufus & Ethel Patrick
Aug. 27	Terry & Joy Keathley
Sep. 17	Henry Hopkins
Sep. 17	Kathleen Gilbreath
Sep. 24	Vannessie Cunningham
Sep. 24	David, Shirley & Michelle Fenn
Sep. 24	Mark Cauble
Oct. 01	Don, Linda & Donnie Mitchell
Oct. 01	Greg Beaty
Oct. 15	Don, Carol & Ken Dodd
Dec. 03	Ken & Gladys Fehling
Dec. 10	Norman, Marie & Ricky Smedley

Total Additions: 62

— 1978 —

Died (2)
Mar. 26 Margaret Slay
Sep. 14 Lee Flowers

Moved Away (35)
Jan.   George Sims family (4)
Jan. 15   Bob, Joan & Carol Oler
Jan.   Dianne Frye
Feb. 01   Ken Springer
Feb. 26   John & Marge Waisanen
Feb. 26   Wade & Constance Coney
Mar. 12   Joyce Resnick
Apr. 02   Jodie Cunningham
May 07   Bill & Irene Lee
June 18   Marilyn Dixon
June 18   Teri Hahn
July 09   Terry & Joy Keathley
July 30   David Palmer
Aug. 13   Hardy family (4)
Aug. 13   Susan Myers
Sep. 03   Alton, Rosie, James & Luci Pribble
Oct. 18   Charles White
Nov.   Holly Hinlicky
Nov. 26   Karen Swartz
Dec. 17   Jim Harris

Total Losses: 52   **206 Families; 384 Members**

— 1979 —

Our spring meeting was conducted by Bill Smith from West Monroe, Louisiana on February 5-9.

The School of Spiritual Development taught by Bill Hatcher began on March 4 with the first thirteen-week courses in intensive Bible training. Classes were held Sunday morning (First John), Tuesday evening (Introductory Survey I), Wednesday morning (First & Second Thessalonians), Wednesday evening (Philippians) and Thursday evening (First Timothy).

The long awaited "Circles of Truth" books by Bill Hatcher were received in April.

New deacons were appointed on April 29. They were Jesse Ford, Hugh Horrocks, Carl Mack and Austen Moore.

On May 10, Jon Hazelip, coach at Alabama Christian College, was the guest speaker for the Parent-Teen Banquet held at the Sweden House.

Rod Rutherford, from Hobart, Tasmania, Australia, spoke to us concerning the work there on June 6.

The annual Junior/Senior Banquet was held in Fort Lauderdale in June. This congregation was well represented in the winners. Chet Brown was chosen King, Julie Hopkins was chosen Queen, and DeRita Hickerson was chosen first runner-up to the Queen. We had fourteen graduating seniors.

Fred Faulkner began a new class for men on June 13 entitled "The Role of Husbands in Marriage."

Wade & Margie Bates began their new work in Astoria, Oregon in July.

Because of poor health, Hayward Milton resigned as elder on July 8.

Due to a volcanic eruption, a large amount of clothing was collected and sent to Saint Vincent on July 8.

Buddy & Jeannie Lawrenson and family arrived in the States from South Africa for a visit in August and returned on November 5.

The second session of the School of Spiritual Development began on September 23 for thirteen weeks. The schedule was the same as the spring classes except for Wednesday morning, when Second Timothy was taught.

The Golden Years Banquet was held December 14 in honor of our senior members.

— 1979 —

Elders
Johnny Davis
Joe Holland
Jerry Hopkins
Harold Keathley
Don Spurlock

Deacons
Gerald Bobo
Pete Brown
Doug Carmack
Jesse Ford
Tom Holaday
Hugh Horrocks
Bill Ingram, Sr.
Dewayne Lanham
Carl Mack
Tom Mitchell
Austen Moore
Bill Powell
Russell Waggoner

Evangelists
William C. Hatcher
Kerry Cain
Dean Reynolds

College
Loni & Chet Brown
Woody & Cyndi Guin
Julie Hopkins
Kerry & Linda Keathley
Phil & Kevin Keathley
Patrick Laconte
Jim Leslie
Teresa Mitchell
Tim Pannell
Mary Ramberg
Alex Ray
Paul Wong

Missionaries
Buddy Lawrenson (South Africa)
Tom Fairley (Tasmania, Australia)
Wade Bates (Astoria, Oregon)
Walter Ashenfelter (South Boston, VA)
Michael Lawler (Wallingford, CT)
Martin Davis (Clarksville, GA)

— 1979 —

Baptized (13)
Feb. 02 Veronica Schofield
Feb. 11 Tyrone Carter
Feb. 26 Latrelle Weldon
Mar. 04 Ana Ellis
Mar. 11 Tonya Greene
Mar. 18 Paul Wong
Apr. 23 Helen Giannone Slay
May 20 Kasandra Gilmore
May 20 Shirley Jean Moore
July 19 Charlene Pavlovsky
Aug. 26 Debra Dunbar
Nov. 07 Kelly Holaday
Dec. 30 Karen Anderson

Identified (16)
Jan. 01 Ted & Kathryn Garrison
Jan. 21 Hattie & Andrea Simpson
Feb. 07 Hank & Mary Flowers
Feb. 11 Steven Ellis
Feb. 25 Debora Patterson
Apr. 15 Mary Orene Harbour
May 13 Linda Joiner
June 06 Greg & Michelle Morris
July 08 Margaret Griffo
Sep. 09 Pearl El
Oct. 28 Ulysses Upshaw
Dec. 23 Tommy Pauldo

Restored (3)
June 03 Cindy Brooks
July 01 Rick & Carole Jenkins

Total Additions: 32

— 1979 —

Died (8)
Mar. 13 Red Johnson
Apr. 09 Thomas Irvine
June 17 Latrelle Weldon
Aug. 26 Sarah Lee
Oct. 08 Charles Hane
Dec. 10 Emma Reeder
Dec. 19 John Price
Dec. 25 William Jackson

Moved Away (21)
Jan. 14 Jim Harris
Feb. 02 Willie & Marie Irvine
Mar. 04 Milo & Merle Watson
Mar. 11 Connie Brooks
Apr. 01 Frank Wineinger
Apr. 01 Maria Nieland
June 17 Linda & Vicki Blass
June 24 Richard & Sue Johnson
July 08 Mildred Moore
Aug. 19 Arthur Thayres
Aug. 20 Greg Beaty
Aug. 26 Charlene Pavlovsky
Aug. 26 Mary Anstis
Sep. 01 Toni Banuelos
Sep. 09 Roger & Sandy Shell
Oct. 21 Ricky Bonk

Moved Membership (1)
Sep. 01 Peg MacDougal

Total Losses: 35   **201 Families; 362 Members**

— 1980 —

Otis Gatewood was our guest speaker on January 20, and $1,106.34 was given to help preach the gospel in countries behind the Iron Curtain.

The third session of the School of Spiritual Development began on March 2. Sunday morning and Wednesday evening, First John was taught; Tuesday evening, Introductory Survey III; Wednesday morning, First Corinthians; and Thursday evening, First Peter.

On April 6, Bob Hare was our guest speaker and an additional $327 was given for work in countries behind the Iron Curtain.

In April, the elders announced that Gary McMahan would arrive in September to direct the Personal Work Program and to work with the teens.

Our spring meeting was held on May 4 with Avon Malone, from Searcy, Arkansas, as the speaker.

The Teen/Parent Banquet was held at the Sweden House on May 16, with Sammy Long, from Lake Butler, Florida, as the speaker.

On June 1, Bill Hatcher terminated his work with this congregation as the regular minister but will continue to teach in the School of Spiritual Development six months each year (March-May and October-December).

Glann M. Lee, from Birmingham, Alabama, was our guest speaker on June 22.

A Congregational Development Seminar was conducted on August 11-15 by brother and sister T.B. Underwood, Jr. from Nashville, Tennessee.

The elders announced in August that Glann M. Lee would arrive in September to begin working as our regular minister.

Kerry & Tommie Cain and family moved to Lake City, Florida on August 22.

Dwight Smith, from Tabernacle, New Jersey, was our guest speaker on August 24.

Gary & Karen McMahan arrived on September 1 and Glann M. Lee and family arrived on September 9.

The fourth session of the School of Spiritual Development began September 21. Titus was taught on Sunday morning and Wednesday evening; Introductory Survey IV, Tuesday evening; First Corinthians, Wednesday morning; and James, Thursday evening.

B. C. Carr and J. Noel Meredith, from the Florida School of Preaching in Lakeland, spoke to us on September 21.

— 1980 —

Jerry Hopkins resigned as elder of this congregation on October 12. He had served as elder since October 1971 and as deacon since 1965.

Two new elders were appointed on November 13. They were William T. Ingram and Dewayne Lanham.

Elders
Johnny B. Davis
Joe D. Holland
William T. Ingram, Sr.
Harold L. Keathley
S. Dewayne Lanham
Donald G. Spurlock

Evangelists
Glann M. Lee
William C. Hatcher
Dean Reynolds

Personal Work/Youth
Gary McMahan

Deacons
Gerald Bobo
Pete Brown
Doug Carmack
Jesse Ford
Tom Holaday
Hugh Horrocks
Carl Mack
Tom Mitchell
Austen Moore
Bill Powell
Russell Waggoner

— 1980 —

Baptized (15)
Apr. 13	Shirley Deihl
Apr. 13	Pam Holaday
Apr. 20	Bobby Cato
Apr. 23	Maryse Kibler
Apr. 27	Kelsenia Spearman
Apr.	Judy Hillerich
May 18	John Palmer
June 29	Debbie Crowell
July 20	Julia Springer
July 20	Reneé Fenn
Aug. 03	Kelly Cain
Oct. 05	Barry Bicknell
Nov. 09	Myrtle Morris
Nov. 10	Therese Parker
Dec. 14	James Keuspert

Restored (2)
June 29	Tim Collier
Nov. 09	William Morris

Identified (28)
Jan. 06	Larry & Bonnie Vargas
Jan. 06	Johnnie Ruth Spearman
Jan. 06	Cedric Wade
Feb. 07	Russell & Ethel Stotler
Feb. 10	Jerry & Jeanie Langford
Mar. 02	John Porteé
Mar. 23	Marsha Leonard
Apr. 06	Carolee Oler
July 13	Frances & Deseret Whitehead
Aug. 10	Roger & Gladys Jackson
Aug. 10	Jack Burkhalter
Aug. 27	Gary & Karen McMahan
Sep. 03	Glann, Craig, Becky & Lisa Lee
Sep. 21	Paul & Melanie Blankenship
Nov. 30	Jim & Judy Howell
Dec. 14	Bob & Joan Oler

Total Additions: 45

— 1980 —

Died (6)
Feb. 04 Garnett Hamm
Feb. 12 Alvin Witt
May 22 Ottis Lawson
May 28 Phyllis Moore
July 08 Gertrude Morris
July 26 Tom Hamm

Moved Away (24)
Feb. 03 Viola Whitacre
Feb. 08 Henry Hopkins
Feb. 10 Kim Knowles
Apr. 20 Martha Moss
Apr. 27 Russell & Ethel Stotler
Apr. 27 Claudia Reese
June 01 John Porteé
June 01 Paul, Dorothy & Greg Kimble
June 01 Fred & Mona Faulkner
June 22 Marsha Leonard
July 06 Veronica Schofield
Aug. 03 Georgia Davis
Aug. 10 Tim Pannell
Aug. 18 Allen & Connie Gunn
Aug. 22 Kerry, Tommie & Kelly Cain
Sep. 21 Melva Naranjo
Nov. 23 Tyrone Carter

Moved Membership (6)
Feb. 10 Lee Wineinger
May 18 Alvie O. Davis
May 18 Phil Wineinger
July 06 Tim & Debbie Collier
July 13 Millie Wineinger

Total Losses: 43   **194 Families; 347 Members**

— 1981 —

In February, this congregation had between 250 and 300 enrolled in a new Bible correspondence course.

Our spring meeting with G.K. Wallace was cancelled because of his health, but another was scheduled for March 29-April 2 with Jim Mankin, from Madison, Tennessee, as the speaker.

The fifth session of the School of Spiritual Development taught by Bill Hatcher began on March 1. "Circles of Truth" was taught on Sunday morning and Wednesday evening; Introductory Survey (5) on Tuesday evening; First Corinthians (3) on Wednesday morning; and James (2) on Thursday evening.

Gary McMahan and family left on May 1 to return to Richardson, Texas. Ron Brackett was appointed youth director with Bill Ingram, Jr. as assistant beginning the first of May.

The annual Junior/Senior Banquet was held in Fort Lauderdale on May 22. Beth Bobo won the award for best theme and was also crowned Queen. Nick Hanna, Jr. tied for King.

Michael Hatcher was our guest speaker on May 24. He presently preaches for the church in Durant, Oklahoma.

Austen Moore resigned as deacon of this congregation on June 1. He had served since April 29, 1979.

Harold Poland from Arvida, California spoke to us Sunday morning, June 28, on the work in Barbados, and Jim Dexter was our guest speaker that evening.

The video tapes on "The Total Commitment Philosophy" were shown here on August 31-September 1. One of the speakers, Lynn Cook, from Miami, was here to answer questions on this subject.

An Adult Bible Class Committee was appointed the first of September to try to improve the attendance and to offer a wider selection of classes from which the adults may choose.

The sixth session of the School of Spiritual Development began September 6. "Circles of Truth" (2) was taught Sunday morning and Wednesday evening; Introductory Survey (6) on Tuesday evening; First Corinthians (4) on Wednesday morning; and Hebrews (1) on Thursday evening.

Don Spurlock resigned as elder on September 20, serving since 1964. Tom Mitchell resigned as deacon on October 14. He served since October 1966.

A special workshop was conducted on November 13-15 by Jack Exum entitled "Three Unusual Days." $2,567 was collected to help with his work.

— 1981 —

For the second year, a group met together on Thursday, November 25 to have Thanksgiving dinner at the building.

Dan Jenkins from Birmingham, Alabama was our guest speaker on November 21. On November 29, the elders announced that he would be coming to work as Personal Work Director in January of 1982.

Elders
Johnny B. Davis
Joe D. Holland
William T. Ingram, Sr.
Harold L. Keathley
S. Dewayne Lanham

Evangelists
Glann M. Lee
William C. Hatcher
Dean Reynolds

Deacons
Gerald Bobo
Pete Brown
Doug Carmack
Jesse Ford
Tom Holaday
Hugh Horrocks
Carl Mack
Bill Powell
Russell Waggoner

— 1981 —

Baptized (27)

Jan. 04	Cleamond Walker
Jan. 04	Ronnie Dean
Jan. 11	Randy Reese
Jan. 13	Janice Reese
Feb. 01	Leesa LeGrand
Feb. 01	Mike Parker
Feb. 16	Paula Summers
Mar. 11	Helen Stocum
Mar. 11	Daren Holaday
Mar. 22	Jud Davis
Mar. 22	Carl Miller
Mar. 30	Shelly Hanna
Mar. 31	Sandy Judd
Mar. 31	Becky Spurlock
Apr. 01	Chuckie Reeves
Apr. 07	Charles Smith
June 28	Kim Shipley
July 19	Jason Howell
July 30	Teresa Palmer
Aug. 02	Kim Langford
Aug. 16	Dawn Fish
Aug. 02	Krikett Harris
Sep. 07	Ernest Baptiste
Sep. 15	Denise Wright
Oct. 02	Lynne Seay
Oct. 04	Ron Levitan
Nov. 29	Dawn Dodd

Identified (28)

Jan. 04	Dan & Jean Kibler
Jan. 04	Tammy Mauney
Jan. 04	Bessie Perry
May 13	Alice & Kara Bevis
May 31	Terry West
July 02	Dewight & Nylene Lanham
July 05	G.R. & Cherrye Fletcher
Aug. 02	Ralph Oler
Aug. 09	Debbie Clemans
Aug. 16	Flossie Harris
Aug. 23	David Palmer
Aug. 30	Irene & Sylvester Williams
Aug. 30	Anita Gouge
Aug. 30	Gwen Lyons
Aug. 30	Kim Yoakam
Sep. 01	Rita & Sterling Frederick
Sep. 13	Doug Lemley
Sep. 20	Claramay Moore
Oct. 11	Mike Manis
Nov. 15	Edith Hill
Nov. 22	Monica Parker
Nov. 29	Eva Brackett

Restored (4)

Aug. 09	Kasandra Gilmore
Nov. 09	Larry Coker
Nov. 16	Nadine Coker
Nov. 29	Linda Nadine Johnson

Total Additions: 59

— 1981 —

Died (5)
Jan. 04 Carl Whitacre
Jan. 12 Rae Roller
May 20 Rufus Patrick
July 27 Charlotte Johnson
Aug. 21 Charles Smith

Moved Away (11)
Jan. 11 Ken & Gladys Fehling
Jan. 11 Paul & Melanie Blankenship
Mar. 22 Carl Miller
Apr.   Edith Burnette Anderson
May 01 Gary & Karen McMahan
June 01 Bessie Perry
June 09 Terri Mitchell
Dec. 29 John Palmer

Moved Membership (9)
Jan. 01 Margrite Price
May 10 Joyce, Andrew, Andrea & Monica Parker
Aug. 16 Jack Burkhalter
Oct.   Kasandra Gilmore
Nov. 01 Ethel Patrick
Dec. 13 Martha Myers

Total Losses: 43 **201 Families; 365 Members**

— 1982 —

Dan Jenkins and his family arrived on January 20 and Dan began his work as personal work director.

Johnny Ramsey conducted our spring meeting on February 14-18.

The seventh session of the School of Spiritual Development taught by Bill Hatcher began March 7. "Prayer, Fasting and Other Questions" was taught Sunday morning and Wednesday evening; Introductory Survey (7) on Tuesday evening; First Corinthians was completed on Wednesday morning; and Hebrews (2) on Thursday evening.

Buddy & Jeannie Lawrenson returned from Cape Town, South Africa on March 31 and remained here until September 1, when they moved to Pekin, Indiana.

An all-day Youth Rally was conducted here on April 17, with Mark Swindall and Dan Jenkins as speakers.

Glann Lee resigned on April 25 and began work with the Northside congregation on May 23.

Tom Holaday resigned as deacon on May 9 and moved to Vero Beach in June.

Peggy Haines was crowned Queen of the Junior/Senior Banquet In Fort Lauderdale in May and Craig Lanham was crowned King. Peggy also won the award for writing the best theme.

Dan Jenkins became the full-time preacher of this congregation on June 6. Bill Hatcher was presented with the IBM Word Processing Computer to help in his writing on June 6.

A new twenty-five lesson Bible correspondence course began on June 20. All members are encouraged to take it.

The final session of the School of Spiritual Development began September 5. "The Beatitudes of The Bible" was taught Sunday morning; Introductory Survey (8) on Tuesday evening; "Singing and the Songs That We Sing" on Wednesday evening; and Hebrews (3) on Thursday evening.

David Fenn, Jack Kline, David Sproule and Scott Studer were appointed deacons on October 31.

A class for potential song leaders began on October 31.

A Creation/Evolution Seminar was conducted by Dr. Bert Thompson on November 5-7.

We began sponsoring Dorothy Stamps at Georgia Christian Home on November 14. Arlene Berry, who we formerly sponsored, no longer needs our help.

— 1982 —

Bill and Peggy Hatcher moved back to Dallas, Texas on December 18.

Elders
Johnny B. Davis
Joe D. Holland
William T. Ingram, Sr.
Harold L. Keathley
S. Dewayne Lanham

Deacons
Gerald Bobo
Pete Brown
Doug Carmack
David Fenn
Jesse Ford
Hugh Horrocks
Jack Kline
Carl Mack
Bill Powell
David Sproule
Scott Studer
Russell Waggoner

Evangelists
Dan Jenkins
Dean Reynolds

College
Paul Binford
Beth Bobo
Chet Brown
Chip Carmack
John Mark Davis
Alisa Fifield
Peggy Haines
Wes Holland
David Jenkins
Debbie Jenkins
Chris Keathley
Patrick LaConte
Craig Lanham
Paula Summers

— 1982 —

Baptized (16)
Mar. 10 Jose Dirube
Apr. 11 Hattie Lee Daniels
Apr. 12 Lisa Morris
Apr. 18 Philip Lee Girten
June 06 Jason Bobo
June 27 Susan Alcock
July 04 Dawn Langford
Aug. 01 April McKinney
Aug. 29 Scott Smith
Sep. 13 Martha Rose Burton
Sep. 19 Marie Maroon
Oct. 17 Courtney Carmack
Oct. 30 Doug Reese
Nov. 21 Betty Harrison
Dec. 01 Mary Stroh
Dec. 05 Ronald Fernander

Restored (1)
June 20 Jerry Hopkins, Jr.

Identified (45)
Jan. 20 Dan & Judie Jenkins (5)
Feb. 28 Martha Myers
Mar. 14 Nancy Dirube
Mar. 14 Sandra Dennard
Mar. 21 Ronda Clark
Mar. 21 Betty Fernander
Mar. 31 Cheryl Reneé Daniels
Apr. 25 Millie Ames
Apr. 25 Reba Little
May 30 Frank Binford family (5)
May 30 Naomi Galyan
May 30 Rae Evans
June 13 Joe Keathley
June 20 Cheryl Tatar
June 20 Ron Kibler
July 04 Richard & Sue Hardin
July 07 Ron & Jane Wiewora
July 14 Darlene Forde
July 14 Ricky & Willie Smith
Aug. 15 Vera Day
Aug. 15 Kevin Wagner
Aug. 22 Connie & Amy West
Aug. 25 Mae Pierce
Aug. 29 Lance, Brenda & Brad Collier
Aug. 29 Kitty Stone
Sep. 05 Shelley Carrin
Sep. 05 Ray Radford
Sep. 12 Audrey Archer
Sep. 12 Greg Beaty
Nov. 14 Isaac & Ruth Burgess

Total Additions: 62

— 1982 —

Died (6)
Feb. 14   Hayward Milton
Mar. 21   Bud Carpenter
May 17   Larry Coker
May 19   Thelma Paulin
July 20   Iris McGarvey
Dec. 31   Mary Tuggle

Moved Away (20)
Jan. 06   Steve & Ana Ellis
Feb. 14   Chuck & Debbie Milton
Apr. 18   Sandra Dennard
Apr. 10   John & Lynn Farrar
May 19   Tom Holaday family (4)
May 23   Glann & Craig Lee
July 28   Austen & Claramay Moore
Sep. 19   Larry & Bonnie Vargas
Dec. 15   Doug Lemley
Dec. 18   Bill & Peggy Hatcher

Total Losses: 34   **225 Families; 397 Members**

— 1983 —

The Alabama Christian College Chorus sang for us following services on Sunday, January 9.

Maxie Boren conducted our meeting on January 23-27. There were five baptisms and five requesting prayers.

Three new deacons were appointed on February 6. They were Don Dodd, Don Hickerson, and Dewight Lanham.

The annual Sweetheart Banquet for our seniors was hosted by the teens on February 12.

On March 12, the young adults held their second Road Rally.

The David Lipscomb College Chorus sang for us on March 16.

The congregation received a progress report from the elders on the Jupiter work on March 27. We saw slides of the property that has been purchased for the building there.

The Parent/Teen Banquet was held on May 6 at Peter's Backyard in North Palm Beach with Jerry Cantrell as the speaker.

The Junior/Senior Banquet was held in Fort Lauderdale on May 20. John Dallas was chosen first runner-up to the King.

On May 13, a Grade School Fellowship was organized and conducted by Jim and Brenda Whitesides.

Ron Brackett resigned as youth director on May 22.

May 28 was truly a "Day of Victory" for Palm Beach Lakes. The members of this congregation painted the entire complex in four hours. We received coverage in local newspapers and on television for our accomplishment.

One of our deacons, Jack Kline, moved away on June 1.

A program for new converts by Dewight Lanham began on June 19.

One of our deacons, Hugh Horrocks, moved away on July 7.

A Newcomers' Banquet was held on July 23 with Kerry Cain as the speaker. He also spoke to us at both services on Sunday, July 24.

The Marriage Enrichment Seminar with Carl Brecheen and Paul Faulkner was conducted on August 5-6. There were 22 congregations represented and 27 local non-members attended.

A Spiritual Enrichment Weekend was conducted by our young adults at the Central Florida Bible Camp facilities September 16-18.

Joe Alcock was appointed as deacon on September 4.

— 1983 —

Bill & Ronda Ingram, Richard & Sue Hardin, John & Sue Hoelzer, and Steve & Jean Lucas were appointed new teen directors on September 25.

Bill Hatcher conducted the School of Spiritual Development during the month of October. Sunday morning and Wednesday night he presented the one chapter books: Philemon, Second John, Third John, and Jude. Tuesday evening he taught Ephesians, and Thursday evening he taught an introduction to Revelation. The enrollment in these classes was the largest ever had.

Monday night visitation began on October 10.

An ice cream supper honoring our elders was held on November 6. They each were presented with a scrapbook containing letters of appreciation from the members.

Elders
Johnny B. Davis
Joe D. Holland
William T. Ingram, Sr.
Harold L. Keathley
S. Dewayne Lanham

Evangelists
Dan Jenkins
Dean Reynolds

Deacons
Joe Alcock
Gerald Bobo
Pete Brown
Doug Carmack
Don Dodd
David Fenn
Jesse Ford
Don Hickerson
Dewight Lanham
Carl Mack
Bill Powell
David Sproule
Scott Studer
Russell Waggoner

— 1983 —

Baptized (40)
Jan. 02   Annette Sproule
Jan. 22   Beatrice Brumfiel
Jan. 26   Pat Weil
Jan. 26   Jonathan Jenkins
Jan. 26   Trina Wright
Jan. 27   Dorothy Ridling
Apr. 10   Dave Holaday
Apr. 24   Mike & Donna Erickson
May 01   Andrea Fernander
May 22   Tim Howard
June 13   Kathe Howard
July 01   Sharon Littlefield
July 27   Tracy Tortoreo
Aug. 03   Steven Morton
Aug. 14   Marylian Ross
Aug. 21   Heather Lanham
Aug. 28   Debbie Reese
Aug. 28   Jimmy Hanna
Aug. 31   Tamara Garcia
Sep. 02   Monica Smith
Sep. 04   Silas Lynch
Sep. 09   Bruce DeMoss
Sep. 14   Vanessa Nelson
Sep. 14   Kim Cato
Oct. 03   Gerald & Beverly Pitts
Oct. 09   Brandon Whitesides
Oct. 14   Glenn Martin
Oct. 16   Douglas Barry
Oct. 17   Marci Barry
Oct. 23   Denise Edwards
Oct. 30   Victor & Sandra Colage
Nov. 09   Linda Christensen
Nov. 09   Kenneth (Buzz) Nelson

Baptized (cont.)
Dec. 05   William & Donna Garland
Dec. 29   Bessie & Marshal Walker

Identified (44)
Jan. 02   Steve & Jean Lucas
Jan. 09   Johnny & Penny Minchey
Jan. 23   Jim & Brenda Whitesides
Feb. 12   John & Sue Hoelzer
Feb. 27   Robert & Jackie Price
Apr. 03   Novel & Mary Brown
Apr. 17   Northmore Hamill
May 08   Rick Tibbetts
May 29   Bentley Utt
June 05   Robert & Mattie Davis
June 26   Dean Williams
July 10   Tom Genduso
July 17   Gary & Cindy LaConte
July 17   Corwin & Patty Snyder
July 31   Tom & Pat Walsh
Aug. 14   Bob & Cindy Young
Aug. 14   Beth Fry
Aug. 24   Dave Payne
Aug. 28   Robert & Pam Medlock
Aug. 31   David Brown
Sep. 04   Bessie Hunt
Sep. 25   Lorine Johnson
Sep. 25   Tom & Bonnilee Kreinberg
Sep. 25   Jeffrey Jacob
Sep. 25   Barbara King
Oct. 16   Hattie Hopkins
Oct. 23   Dwight Clemans
Nov. 06   Bart & Helen Ritter
Nov. 13   Mary Blue Conner

Total Additions: 86

— 1983 —

Identified (cont.)
Dec. 25   Kevin & Karen Keathley

Restored (1)
June 12   Judy Gentry

Died (1)
Oct. 12   Carol Oler

Moved Away (18)
Mar. 20   Trillis Collier
Apr. 24   Eva Brackett
May 08   Jeff Lanham
June 01   Jack & Mildred Kline
June 05   Marie Maroon Shiver
June 05   Kitty Stone
June 12   April McKinney
June 27   Ricky Smith
July 07   Hugh & Linda Horrocks
Aug. 10   Tim & Debbie Cox
Oct. 26   Greg Beaty
Oct. 30   Victor Banuelos
Nov. 16   Tracy Tortoreo
Nov. 27   Boots Wood
Dec. 28   Dean Williams

Moved Membership (4)
Mar. 06   Don, Linda & Donnie Mitchell
Nov. 02   Phil Keathley

Total Losses: 36   **248 Families; 447 Members**

— 1984 —

Bruce DeMoss left on January 18 to begin his studies at the Memphis School of preaching in Memphis, Tennessee.

Steve & Ana Ellis arrived on January 29 to work full-time with this congregation following his graduation from Memphis School of Preaching.

The annual Sweetheart Banquet for our older members was held on February 11 hosted by the teens.

Our spring meeting was held on February 19-23 with Willard Collins as the speaker. Our record Sunday morning attendance was 635, with records being broken at every service.

The annual Road Rally was held by the Young Adults on May 5.

Jesse Ford resigned as deacon on May 6. He had served this congregation as an elder, deacon and area coordinator at different times during 1973-1984. His health made this decision necessary.

Dan began a series of special lessons on May 13 entitled "Seven Steps to Divorce Court."

The Junior/Senior Banquet was held on May 18. Matthew Binford was selected King. Ken Dodd was first runner-up to the King and also won the award for best theme.

Don & Jane McWhorter were with us on June 1-3. Don spoke at the Newcomers' Banquet on Friday night, and there were special classes on Saturday taught by both Don (for the men) and Jane (for the women).

Jay Winter left on June 17 to attend Memphis School of Preaching.

Our second Spiritual Enrichment Weekend was held on September 14-16 at the Central Florida Bible Camp. Over 100 of our members attended.

Jeff Leslie and Marion (Red) Springer were appointed deacons on September 23.

The long-awaited Jupiter/Tequesta work began on October 7. Steve Ellis was selected as the minister and forty-seven members from Palm Beach Lakes became the nucleus for this congregation including two of our elders, William T. Ingram and Dewayne Lanham, and two of our deacons, Gerald Bobo and Dewight Lanham.

Bill Hatcher was our guest speaker on October 21.

Joe Ruiz was guest speaker on October 24, and $1,144 was contributed toward his work in China.

Don Hickerson was ordained as an elder on October 28.

The Creation/Evolution Seminar was conducted on November 2-4 by

— 1984 —

Dr. Bert Thompson from Montgomery, Alabama.

Jim Whitesides was appointed deacon on November 11.

The organization meeting for the "Keenage" program was held on Tuesday morning, November 27.

New area boundaries were announced on December 2 with new area coordinators to be announced later.

December 9 was "Coming Home" Sunday. Every former member known to be in the area was contacted by letters and encouraged to attend, especially this day.

Elders
Johnny B. Davis
Don R. Hickerson
Joe D. Holland
Harold L. Keathley

Deacons
Joe Alcock
Pete Brown
Doug Carmack
Don Dodd
David Fenn
Jeff Leslie
Carl Mack
Bill Powell
Marion Springer
David Sproule
Scott Studer
Russell Waggoner
Jim Whitesides

Evangelists
Dan Jenkins
Dean Reynolds

Began Work in Jupiter (October 7)
Gerald, Susan & Jason Bobo
D-D, Bobby & Kim Cato
Steve & Ana Ellis
Mary Fields
Odell Fields
G.R. & Cherrye Fletcher
Woody & Cyndi Guin
Bill & Helen Hamilton
Josie Hamilton
Bill & Inell Ingram
Bill & Ronda Ingram
Tom, Bonnilee & Heidi Kreinberg
Dan & Jean Kibler
James & Elaine Kuespert
Jerry, Jeanie, Kim & Dawn Langford
Dewayne, Rita, Craig & Heather Lanham
Dwight & Nylene Lanham
Tom, Frankie & Mike Mitchell
Bob & Joan Oler
Robert & Jackie Price
Ron & Jane Wiewora

— 1984 —

Baptized (47)

Jan. 03	Deboria Faye Walker
Jan. 03	Charles Walker
Jan. 15	Mike Lang
Jan. 29	Brady & Karin Neeld
Jan. 29	Bobby Ingraham
Jan. 30	Angela Walker
Jan. 30	Lillian Bankston
Jan. 31	Joy Dean Harper
Feb. 08	Mavadell Gardner
Feb. 06	Carol Foster
Feb. 13	Rose Mary West
Feb. 13	Martha Rose Burton
Feb. 16	Kristy Christensen
Feb. 19	Norris Heard
Feb. 22	Paul Cable
Feb. 23	Sheila Joiner
Feb. 29	Vincent & Yvonne Rogers
Mar. 04	Heidi Kreinberg
Mar. 19	Cynthia Walker (Ingraham)
Mar. 28	Bud Anderson
Mar. 29	Rowena Lynch
Apr. 05	Charlie Eaton, Jr.
Apr. 08	Scotty Studer
Apr. 08	Jennifer Anderson
Apr. 09	Becky Townsend
Apr. 15	Joseph & Janice Maloney
Apr. 19	Julie Thomas
Apr. 22	Nita DeVore (Manis)
May 09	Kirk O'Neal
May 12	Micky Affron
June 01	Kipp Affron
June 18	Brenda Harris
June 27	Mike Gygi
July 17	Jered Primicerio
July 17	Faye Wilson
July 18	Michael Ferguson
July 25	Dale Clayton
Aug. 26	Kristi Schmidt
Sep. 24	Robin Xaros
Oct. 01	Kenny Hirsh
Oct. 28	John R. Thomas
Dec. 02	Ross Givens & Terrell Baker
Dec. 30	Lance Teachworth

Identified (33)

Jan. 15	Forrest, Eunice & Jack Heflin
Jan. 29	Steve & Ana Ellis
Feb. 08	Emily Peterson
Mar. 04	Dan & Luann McLeod
Mar. 04	Dennis & Ann Carter
May 27	Angellia Twiggs
June 03	Odell Fields
July 08	Robert, Juanetta & Frances Walker
July 08	Doris & Cheryl Middleton
July 08	Ida Morgan
July 08	David E. Brown
Aug. 05	David & Elizabeth Brown
Sep. 16	Rudolph Gordon
Sep. 19	Paula Jo Carpenter
Sep. 23	Tim Collier
Oct. 07	Gladys Daniel
Oct. 07	John, Nancie & Kevin Strobeck
Nov. 04	Kathy Clemmons
Nov. 18	Fred & Tammy Battistic
Nov. 25	Tinker & Amy Stewart

Total Additions: 86

— 1984 —

Restored (5)
Aug. 29 Judy Hillerich
Oct. 28 Jerry Hopkins, Jr.
Nov. 04 Norris Rutledge
Nov. 18 Tom Slater
Dec. 09 Cherie Hanna

Died (4)
Jan. 23 Cecil Bone
Apr. 13 Helen Stocum
Oct. 03 Judy Portz
Dec. 20 Tom Slater

Moved Away (23)
Jan. 18 Bruce DeMoss
Feb. 15 Mavadell Gardner
May 18 Peggy Haines Hall
June 08 Milt & Nicki Wickles
June 08 Jay & Betty Winter
June 10 Gary & Cindy LaConte
July 01 Richard & Sue Hardin
July 15 Nick Hanna, Jr.
July 18 Michael Ferguson
July 22 Norris Heard
Sep. 16 Judy Hillerich
Sep. 17 Kirk O'Neal
Oct. 14 Ron & Maryse Kibler
Oct. 21 Steve & Jean Lucas
Nov. 25 Dave Payne
Dec. 02 Russ Givens & Terrall Baker

Began Work in Jupiter (October 7)
See Page 49

Total Losses: 93   **248 Families; 437 Members**

— 1985 —

A dinner for all ladies of the congregation was held at the building on January 11.

The annual Sweetheart Banquet honoring our senior members was held by the teens on February 16.

Many of our members helped to paint the home of Pat & Janet Weil in Lake Park and to do other needed repairs in February.

The pictorial directories were ready in March.

Our spring meeting was conducted on March 10-14 with Tom Holland as the speaker.

Dan Jenkins delivered a series of lessons on Matthew 24 in April.

The annual Young Adult sponsored Road Rally was held on April 20.

Our Third Annual Ladies' Day was on April 25 with six speakers from this congregation: Aileen Belden, Evelyn Coleman, Loni Brown, June Haines, Judie Jenkins and Joy Judd. Over 100 area women attended.

In May, Dan Jenkins delivered a series of lessons on the Holy Spirit.

The annual Junior/Senior Banquet was held on May 17 in Miami. Connie Sproule was selected Queen and Danny Jenkins as King. Danny also won the award for best theme.

The Parent/Teen Banquet was held on May 31.

On June 30, Dave Holaday, Jim Howell, Dan McLeod, Jerry Pittman, and Jim Rogers were appointed as deacons.

Homecoming services were conducted on July 14 commemorating twenty years in this building. Bill Hatcher and Kerry Cain were the speakers. All former members were invited to attend.

The Spiritual Enrichment Weekend was held at the Lions' Camp in Lake Wales on September 13-15 with about 125 attending.

— 1985 —

Elders
Johnny B. Davis
Don R. Hickerson
Joe D. Holland
Harold L. Keathley

Evangelists
Dan Jenkins
Dean Reynolds

Deacons
Joe Alcock
Pete Brown
Doug Carmack
Don Dodd
David Fenn
Dave Holaday
Jim Howell
Jeff Leslie
Dan McLeod
Carl Mack
Jerry Pittman
Bill Powell
Jim Rogers
Marion Springer
David Sproule
Scott Studer
Russell Waggoner
Jim Whitesides

— 1985 —

Baptized (47)

Jan. 13	Carolyn Tippins
Jan. 13	Edna Williams
Jan. 20	Damaris & Tom Parramore
Feb. 02	Laura Boone
Feb. 03	Greg Brown
Mar. 11	Marie Ruff
Mar. 12	Mary Fernandes
Mar. 12	Traci Bowman
Mar. 13	David Frantz
Mar. 13	Tammy Heath
Mar. 14	Bill Kay
Mar. 16	Jim Boone
Mar. 17	Brenda Nestor
Mar. 17	Robert Walker, Jr.
Apr. 06	Matt McCreary
Apr. 06	Brenda Wood
Apr. 21	Lara Huffman
Apr. 22	Dianne Halenda
June 11	David Bowman
June 13	Ruth Nelson
June 13	Dessie Smith
July 28	Eva Bullard
July 28	Daryl Gordon
Aug. 04	Richard McMasters
Aug. 24	Steve Bedard
Aug. 26	Penny Williams
Aug. 29	Lisa Marquez
Sep. 09	Rick Carter
Sep. 11	Gene Williams
Sep. 12	Jody Massey
Sep. 15	Rich Murphy
Sep. 26	Herman Smith
Oct. 16	Daniel Fuller
Oct. 20	Ruby Terrell, Pam & Ronald
Oct. 20	Marcus D. Hunt
Oct. 23	Gerald Smith
Oct. 27	Jim Howard
Nov. 06	Becky Brackett
Nov. 10	Donna Steward
Nov. 17	Donna Covington
Nov. 25	Betty Bryant
Nov. 27	Johnny Young
Nov. 27	Norma Guthrie Young
Dec. 04	Lucy Young

— 1985 —

Identified (33)

Mar. 03 Norma Ealy
Mar. 14 Nina Smith
Mar. 17 Madella Scott
Mar. 24 Donald & Christine Henderson
Mar. 24 Brian Lewis
Apr. 07 Jose & Nancy Dirube
May 19 Abby Murrell
May 19 Lee Luther Glaze
June 02 John, Marguerite & Paul Kachouroff
June 02 Bill Bollman, Lois, Beulah, Bill Jr. & Ronald
June 23 Dayton Smith
June 23 Anita Gouge
June 23 Kitty Stone
June 30 Jack & Jerry Hoelzer
July 10 Rand E. & Maggie Morgan
July 10 Virginia Brightwell
Sep. 11 Brenda Brown
Sep. 22 Debbi Mengel
Oct. 13 Lula Hill
Oct. 13 Mark Ware
Nov. 24 Rachael Pearson
Dec. 01 Sirpa Armstrong
Dec. 08 Aldene Carvin

Total Additions: 80   **252 Families; 439 Members**

— 1985 —

Moved Away (39)

Jan. 14   Fred & Tammy Battistic
Jan. 23   Mike Gygi
Jan. 23   John Thomas
Mar. 18   Greg Brown
Apr. 07   David & Liz Brown
Apr. 28   Mary Fernandes
May 15   Bob & Cindy Young
May 15   Corwin & Patty Snyder
June 02   Patrice LaConte
July 21   Ann Carter
July 24   Tinker & Amy Stewart
Aug. 04   Monica Maloney
Aug. 09   Kathleen Gilbreath
Aug. 19   James Weil
Aug. 27   Bill, Lois & Ronald Bollman
Sep. 15   Bill Bollman, Jr. & Beulah
Sep. 25   Bob, Joy & Sandy Judd
Oct. 30   Tim & Kathe Howard
Oct. 30   Bill Kay
Nov. 10   Scott & Debbie Smith
Nov. 17   Cedric Wade
Nov. 17   John Mark Davis
Nov. 17   Ron & Linda Levitan
          & Sheila Joiner
Dec. 01   Rick Carter
Dec. 04   Janna Hopkins
Dec. 21   Betty Bryant
Dec. 25   David Bowman

Died (5)

Mar. 01   Ray Evans
Mar. 23   Em Willard
July 06   Dennis Carter
Aug. 10   Northmore Hamill
Nov. 11   F.C. (Doc) Hopkins

Moved Membership (14)

Mar. 24   Lynne Seay
May 15   Rick & Sherrie Tibbetts &
          Karen, Bud & Jennifer
          Anderson
May 15   Terry West
July 07   Kevin & Karen Keathley
Sep. 08   Ida Morgan
Oct. 2   Victor & Mary Jane Rohrer
Nov. 24   Brian Lewis
Dec. 08   Kathy Clemmons

Total Losses: 87   **252 Families; 439 Members**

— 1986 —

Our spring meeting was conducted on January 19-23 with Goebel Music as the speaker. There were three baptisms.

Harold Keathley resigned as elder of this congregation on January 25, after serving in that capacity since August 30, 1970.

Bruce & Lisa DeMoss arrived on February 2 to work with this congregation for a while following his graduation from Memphis School of Preaching.

The annual Sweetheart Banquet hosted by the teens to honor our senior members was held on February 15.

The TLC Workshop was conducted by Carol Dodd & Kim Leslie on April 19. About fifty ladies came to learn how to teach young children more effectively.

The annual Road Rally was held on April 26.

Courtney Carmack won the award for best theme at the Junior/Senior Banquet on May 9.

Jay Winter graduated from Memphis School of Preaching, and he and his family came to work with us on June 29.

The Parent/Teen Banquet was held on June 29.

On July 27, Mike Erickson was appointed as a deacon, and Jerry Hopkins and Doug Carmack were ordained as elders.

The Marriage Enrichment Seminar with Carl Breechen and Paul Faulkner was conducted on August 8-9.

A dinner to honor the Pioneers was sponsored by the young adults on November 1 at the home of Chuck and Mary Reeves.

Our hearts were saddened December 16 when Bill Hatcher passed away following a six-month long bout with lung cancer in Dallas, Texas. Bill worked with this congregation from December 1968 to December 1982.

— 1986 —

Elders
Doug W. Carmack
Johnny B. Davis
Don R. Hickerson
Joe D. Holland
Jerry D. Hopkins

Evangelists
Dan Jenkins
Dean Reynolds
Bruce DeMoss
Jay Winter

Deacons
Joe Alcock
Pete Brown
Don Dodd
Mike Erickson
David Fenn
Dave Holaday
Jim Howell
Jeff Leslie
Dan McLeod
Carl Mack
Jerry Pittman
Bill Powell
Jim Rogers
Marion Springer
David Sproule
Scott Studer
Russell Waggoner
Jim Whitesides

— 1986 —

Baptized (40)

Jan. 05	Austin Lee Williams, Jr.
Jan. 05	Raymond Charles
Jan. 08	David Lawrence
Jan. 20	Gladys Hanna
Jan. 22	Kevin Joy
Jan. 23	Keith Joy
Feb. 02	Evelio Escarria
Mar. 12	Carol Wilson
Mar. 16	Andrew Fox
Mar. 17	George Williams, Jr.
Mar. 23	Chip Stroh
Apr. 01	Lisa Beltran
Apr. 01	Jimi Applegate
Apr. 04	Mary Eutsey
Apr. 14	Roy Neil Smith
May 01	Nick Troy
May 11	Joyce Green
June 23	Ron Dunlap
June 25	Todd & Carol Mackey
June 29	Diane Joy
June 29	William Wedge
July 27	Andrew Mills
Aug. 06	Lonnie Smith
Aug. 15	Charles Middleton
Aug. 17	Allen Goulet
Aug. 24	Tony James Wilson, Jr.
Aug. 31	Beth Whitesides
Sep. 07	David Sproule, II
Sep. 16	Nanette Nunes
Sep. 21	Steven Carmack
Oct. 02	Loretta Holaday
Oct. 05	Carol Gray
Oct. 07	Priscilla Smyth
Dec. 07	Chris Fry
Dec. 14	Debi Alcock
Dec. 19	Harry Lee Harris
Dec. 21	Angelique Stubblefield
Dec. 21	Vivian Brown
Dec. 21	Joseph Maloney, Jr.

— 1986 —

Identified (44)

Jan. 05	Rick & Peggy Hall
Jan. 12	Tim & Debbie Cox
Jan. 20	Rachel Hunnicutt
Jan. 26	Pam Edwards
Feb. 02	Pat Warman
Feb. 02	Doug & Vicky Wiley
Feb. 02	Bruce & Lisa DeMoss
Feb. 09	Lynette Temple
Feb. 16	Polly Carpenter
Feb. 23	Jim & Sheree Kilpatrick
Feb. 23	Randy Yost
Feb. 23	David & Linda Mills
Mar. 09	Ande Fox
Mar. 16	Dean Green
Apr. 16	Wiley Price
Apr. 20	Kevin & Karen Keathley
Apr. 27	Herman & Belle Moody
May 11	Gladys Jackson
May 18	Rodona Smith
June 01	John Jackson
June 01	Janna Hopkins
June 08	Stephen Beliech
June 29	Jay & Betty Winter
Aug. 24	Pauline Vinson
Aug. 31	Ephriam Davis
Sep. 07	Lara Prairie
Sep. 21	Kurt & Joyce Swanson
Oct. 19	Woody & Cyndi Guin
Nov. 16	Bernard Card
Nov. 30	Stella Spurlock
Dec. 21	Maureen Machan
Dec. 28	Larry Brown
Dec. 31	Pat Myers

Restored (14)

Jan. 29	Joe Hanna
Mar. 09	Trudy Seavey Yost
Apr. 20	Carrie Walker
May 07	John R. Thomas
May 18	Vicki Dunlap
May 25	Lorraine Allen
June 08	H. R. Smith
July 16	Lara Huffman
July 20	Rodney Atkisson
July 23	Marilyn Ragin Altidor
July 27	Deborah Moore
Aug. 10	Julie Oldham
Sep. 14	Reba Little
Dec. 21	Larry Brown

Total Additions: 98   **286 Families; 472 Members**

— 1986 —

Died (3)
Aug. 03   Doris Middleton
Dec. 03   Forrest Heflin
Dec. 20   Harry Lee Harris

Moved Away (19)
Jan. 05   Raymond Charles
Jan. 19   Lora Joiner
Apr. 09   Marie Ruff
Apr. 15   Lisa Beltran
June 15   Pam Edwards
June 18   Jerry Hopkins, Jr.
June 18   Andrew Fox
June 29   Ron & Vicky Dunlap
July 06   Richard Murphy
July 09   Jimi Applegate
Aug. 03   John R. Thomas
Aug. 20   Stephen Beliech
Aug. 31   Roger & Gladys Jackson
Aug. 31   Brady & Karin Neeld
Oct. 05   Roy Neil & Rodona Smith

Moved Membership (9)
Apr. 20   Pat Warman
Apr. 20   Sirpa Armstrong
May 21   Randy & Trudy Yost
May 21   Lynette Temple
July 13   John, Nancie & Kevin Strobeck
Aug. 10   Rosemary Laconte

Total Losses: 45   286 Families; 472 Members

— 1987 —

The teens treated the Young Adults with babysitting for their children on January 30 so they could have a "Date Nite."

Bruce & Lisa DeMoss left in January to begin work with the church in Kenton, Ohio.

The annual Sweetheart Banquet given by the teens to honor our senior members was held on Saturday, February 13.

The budget for this year was presented to the congregation on February 15. It will require $7,100 per week.

Future plans for this congregation were announced on February 22. Property on Leo Lane has been acquired. We hope to build within the next few years.

A visitation work party was held on February 28. All visitors to our services within the last year were personally invited to our upcoming meeting.

Our spring meeting was conducted on March 8-12 with Neale Pryor of Searcy, Arkansas as the speaker. We had a record attendance of 650 Sunday morning.

The Pioneers hosted a dinner for the Young Adults on March 24.

Our Fifth Annual Ladies' Day was held on April 23, with Shirley Hopkins and Pat Brown as the speakers. Lunch was provided for about one hundred in attendance.

At the Junior/Senior Banquet in May, Jud Davis was chosen King and Annette Sproule was chosen Queen.

During the summer months, when the regular singing practice was not being held, Dan Jenkins conducted a "pew-packers" class for the children at 6:00 p.m. on Sunday evenings.

The Spiritual Enrichment Weekend was conducted on September 11-13 at the Lion's Camp in Lake Wales.

Sunday evening, October 4, our entire service was conducted by nine of our young men. They led the prayers, conducted the singing, and did the speaking. They did a great job.

Dr. Bert Thompson was here for another Creation/Evolution Seminar on November 13-15.

One of our deacons, Red Springer, resigned this year due to health issues.

— 1987 —

Elders
Doug W. Carmack
Johnny B. Davis
Don R. Hickerson
Joe D. Holland
Jerry D. Hopkins

Evangelists
Dan Jenkins
Dean Reynolds
Jay Winter

Deacons
Joe Alcock
Pete Brown
Don Dodd
Mike Erickson
David Fenn
David Holaday
Jim Howell
Jeff Leslie
Dan McLeod
Carl Mack
Jerry Pittman
Bill Powell
Jim Rogers
David Sproule
Scott Studer
Russell Waggoner
Jim Whitesides

— 1987 —

Baptized (33)

Jan. 11	Thomas & Anita Pugh
Jan. 25	Silas Johnson
Feb. 22	Adam Crandall
Feb. 25	Ashlee Hirsh
Mar. 08	Mark Thompson
Mar. 10	Joyce Barnhouse
Apr. 17	Irene Morlock
Apr. 26	Gene Puckett
Apr. 29	Greg Crandall
May 05	Leigh Luckett
June 06	Doug Lambert
June 09	Gayenell Walker
June 11	Lois Lail
July 01	Cheryl Floyd
July 01	Karen Walter
July 26	Jackie Scourtas
Aug. 02	Robert Medlock, Jr.
Aug. 02	Shane Studer
Aug. 11	Jim & Pam Gibson
Sep. 14	Donna Card
Sep. 15	Dana Barnhouse
Sep. 22	Owen Miley, Jr.
Oct. 04	Kristen Collier
Oct. 15	Tom & Francell McEaddy
Oct. 21	Chris Kachouroff
Nov. 15	Eddie Platt
Nov. 18	Tammy Platt
Nov. 22	Christine Jenkins
Nov. 29	Diane Cole
Dec. 20	Megan Cox

Identified (38)

Jan. 11	Lillie Hill
Jan. 11	Patricia Copeland
Jan. 25	Kathy Johnson
Mar. 15	Chuck & Debbie Milton
Apr. 26	Erma Hill
May 06	Tommy Matthews
May 10	Rhonda Brookins
May 27	Kathy DuBois
June 21	Chip & Julie Carmack
July 01	John Mitchell, III
July 01	Carolyn Tippins
July 19	Alvy Davidson
July 19	Tom Chadwick
July 26	Vidal Villarreal
Aug. 16	Lane & Molly Johnson
Aug. 16	Stephanie Miller
Aug. 23	Craig & LaJuanna Lanham
Aug. 23	Stacey & Darlene Rambold
Aug. 30	Becky Clement
Sep. 13	George & Betty Gean
Sep. 23	Deidra Miley
Sep. 27	Tom, Linda, & Ashanti Brown
Oct. 04	Wayne, June, & Spurgeon Putnam
Oct. 14	Wendy Friedman
Oct. 18	Stan & Sara Bronson
Nov. 01	Janice Hill
Nov. 29	Don Wills

Restored (5)

Jan. 18.	Teri Jenkins
Apr. 26	Lara Huffman
May 17	Charles Walker
Aug. 02	Beverly Owens
Oct. 18	Victor Banuelos

Total Additions: 76

— 1987 —

Died (8)
Feb. 22 Everett Hatfield
Feb. 28 Martha Myers
Mar. 18 Pat Weil
Apr. 07 Jack Hoelzer
Oct. 17 Vern Morris
Oct. 18 Charles & Gayenell Walker
Nov. 02 Willie Townsend

Moved Away (13)
Jan. 31 Bruce & Lisa DeMoss
Apr. 12 Stella Spurlock
June 02 Paula Carpenter
June 13 Dayton Smith
June 24 Jim & Sheree Kilpatrick
July 22 Tony, Doris & Jered Primicerio
Aug. 02 Courtney Carmack
Dec. 02 Rhonda Brookins
Dec. 20 Lillie Hill

Moved Membership (17)
Jan. 25 Matt Binford
Mar. 01 Rachel Hunnicutt Russo
Mar. 01 Pauline Vinson
Mar. 15 David, Linda & Andrew Mills
Apr. 01 Steve Bedard
Apr. 01 Larry, Vivian & Louise Brown
June 24 Frank, Leah, & Jon Binford
June 24 Naomi Galyan
July 22 Tony James Wilson, Jr.
Oct. 21 Kurt & Joyce Swanson

Total Losses: 56   291 Families; 501 Members

— 1988 —

Our spring meeting was conducted on January 17-22 with Maxie Boren as the speaker. This was Maxie's fourth meeting with this congregation.

The first of several Bible School workshops was held on January 30 to prepare visual aids for Bible classes.

The annual Sweetheart Banquet for the Pioneers by the teens was on February 13.

The elders challenged the congregation on February 14 to pay for the property on Leo Lane.

On March 6, Bob Medlock and Greg Morris were appointed deacons.

A special contribution was collected toward the purchase of the Leo Lane property on March 13 of over $100,000.

The Sixth Annual Palm Beach Lakes Ladies' Day was held on April 21 with Peggy Hatcher and Tommie Cain as the speakers. Over two hundred attended. It was the first meeting to be held at night.

The annual Palm Beach Lakes Grand Prix-Road Rally was on April 23.

During the summer months, while the 6:00 p.m. Sunday evening singing class was dismissed, a number of special classes were conducted: a pew-packers class by Dan Jenkins and other classes on benevolence, song leading, area leaders, audio, preparing the Lord's Supper, welcome desk, ushering, and others taught by deacons.

Our New Members' Banquet was held on May 27 with Kerry Cain as the speaker.

Chris Kachouroff was selected King and Dawn Dodd was selected Queen of the Junior/Senior Banquet on May 13. Dawn also won the award for best theme.

One of our deacons, Bob Medlock, passed away on May 31.

B.J. Naylor from Freed-Hardeman College conducted a Teachers' Training Workshop on Friday-Sunday, August 12-14.

Doug Carmack resigned as an elder on August 14 for personal reasons.

A singing school was conducted by Clifford Smith from Selma, Alabama on September 19-22.

Four additional deacons were appointed on September 25: Ron Brackett, Stan Bronson, Joseph Maloney and Chuck Milton.

A special contribution was given in October for the victims of a hurricane in Jamaica.

— 1988 —

The Sonshine Singers from Freed-Hardeman College sang for us on October 1.

Spiritual Enrichment Weekend was conducted on October 21-23 at the Lion's Camp in Lake Wales.

Training for Living classes were conducted on November 13-16 on the themes: Daily Bread from the Word, Daily Devotions in the Word, Daily Challenges from the World, Daily Walk in the World. There were multiple classes each night, being taught on Sunday evening through Wednesday evening.

The teens had a Holiday Dinner for all widows at the home of Dan and Judie Jenkins on December 10.

Bible Class Emphasis Day and a picnic was on December 11.

Elders
Johnny B. Davis
Don R. Hickerson
Joe D. Holland
Jerry D. Hopkins

Evangelists
Dan Jenkins
Dean Reynolds
Jay Winter

Deacons
Joe Alcock
Ron Brackett
Stan Bronson
Pete Brown
Don Dodd
Mike Erickson
David Fenn
Dave Holaday
Jim Howell
Jeff Leslie
Dan McLeod
Carl Mack
Joseph Maloney
Chuck Milton
Greg Morris
Jerry Pittman
Bill Powell
Jim Rogers
David Sproule
Scott Studer
Russell Waggoner
Jim Whitesides

— 1988 —

Baptized (27)
Feb. 14 Sydney Wingate
Mar. 13 Richard & Linda Longhenry
Apr. 07 Stuart Lynch
Apr. 17 Angel Joy
Apr. 19 Michael Small
May 12 Benny & Sarah Rodgers
May 19 Danny King
May 29 Roy Crocker, Jr.
June 26 Jose Martinez
July 10 Bryan Niles
July 28 Corinne Holaday
July 29 Kathy Conner
Sep. 04 Jeanette James
Sep. 10 Susan Joy
Sep. 12 Steven Reeves
Sep. 14 Frances Sargies
Oct. 09 Robyn Medlock
Oct. 12 Louise Barnes
Oct. 23 Sarah Terwillegar
Oct. 29 Debbie Huard
Nov. 02 Nicole Colage
Nov. 06 Janice Wedge
Nov. 27 Dorothy Richter
Nov. 27 Stephanie Pervola
Nov. 30 Justin Collier

Identified (21)
Jan. 10 Edward Barnes
Feb. 07 Michael Mitchell
Mar. 06 Bobby & Kim Knowles
Mar. 20 Don & Wanda Norwood
May 01 Pamela Edwards
May 22 Pat Gonzales

Identified (cont.)
June 29 Scott Joy
Aug. 03 Vandine Montgomery
Sep. 07 David & Beth Marler
Sep. 07 Skye McLeod
Sep. 11 Darrell Young
Oct. 02 Ed Ohlenkamp
Oct. 19 Jim & Mary Moores
Oct. 26 Amos & Marilou Shiver
Nov. 20 C.H. & Lottie Suddreth

Restored (9)
Jan. 06 Trent Hanna
Jan. 10 Frank Wayne Ward
Jan. 17 Thelma Miller
Apr. 10 Rich Murphy
Apr. 17 Bobbi Ferland
June 19 Iralee & Carol Perrine
Nov. 06 Eugene Edwards
Dec. 18 Lynn Blaisdell

Births
Jan. 12 Justin Ryan Smith
Mar. 24 Christopher Jon Keathley
Mar. 27 Heather Leann Longhenry
June 17 Cory Douglas Brown
Aug. 05 Stephan Starling Lynch
Aug. 09 Lance Thomas Jenkins
Aug. 15 Michael Clarence Crandall

Total Additions: 57

— 1988 —

Died (8)
Jan. 07   Bill Sproule
Jan. 14   Elizabeth Thomas
Jan. 17   Tom McEaddy
Jan. 19   Alvy Davidson
May 31   Bob Medlock
June 17   Rodney Atkisson
Aug. 11   Silas Johnson
Oct. 21   Harvey Fort

Moved Away (30)
Jan. 02   Julie Oldham
Jan. 17   Jim & Kim Leslie
Feb. 09   Wayne, June & Spurgeon Putnam
Mar. 30   Donald & Christine Henderson
Apr. 21   Janice Hill
Apr. 21   Ted & Kathryn Garrison
May 08   Rich Murphy
June 19   Don Wills
July 16   Lance Teachworth
July 27   Kathy Johnson
July 30   Loretta Holaday
Aug. 14   Bryan Niles
Aug. 16   Doug & Vicki Wiley
Aug. 28   Mark & Janna Thompson
Aug. 31   Lorraine Allen
Sep. 21   Reba Little
Sep. 30   Rand E & Maggie Morgan
Oct. 09   James Weil
Oct. 14   Jose & Nancy Dirube
Nov. 28   Lonnie & Josephine Foster

Moved Membership (5)
May 29   George & Betty Gean
Aug. 14   Scott Joy
Oct. 30   Mary Stroh
Dec. 07   Vidal Villarrpal

Total Losses: 68   **283 Families; 490 Members**

— 1989 —

This congregation provided workers in the church booth at the South Florida Fair on January 25-February 5.

Effective February 5, Joe Holland became our first full-time elder, taking on the responsibility of visitation, encouraging weak members, and counseling, in addition to his other duties as a elder.

The annual Sweetheart Banquet for the Pioneers hosted by the teens was on February 11.

Our meeting with Johnny Ramsey was conducted on March 5-9, during which we had a record attendance of 665 for morning worship.

The Seventh Ladies' Day was held on April 20 with Mona Faulkner, who now lives in Texas, as the speaker.

Involvement Sunday was on April 23. At the picnic at Dreher Park following morning services, the deacons had areas designated where they could explain their duties and answer questions about their work.

At the Junior/Senior Banquet in Fort Lauderdale on April 28, Jimmy Hanna was selected second runner-up to the King.

The Eighth Annual Road Rally was held on May 27.

The Parent/Teen Banquet honoring our graduating seniors was conducted on June 11.

The Training for Living Classes were conducted on July 30-August 2. During these four nights, sixteen classes were taught by members of this congregation on important subjects. Attendance was good.

"Coming Home" Sunday was on August 20. Invitations were sent to every former member of the church living in this area for whom we had addresses. Several attended, and later in the year, three were restored.

On September 15-17, Wayne Jackson conducted a seminar, "Can the Bible Be Trusted?"

The Sonshine Singers from Freed-Hardeman College sang for us on October 7.

Our Spiritual Enrichment Weekend at the Lion's Club in Lake Wales was on October 20-22.

Jay Winter began a Thursday evening class on Bible Basics in November.

Bill & Inell Ingram opened their home for everyone who wanted to attend Thanksgiving with them this year. They also hosted a singing for anyone in the congregation in December.

— 1989 —

Elders
Johnny B. Davis
Don R. Hickerson
Joe D. Holland
Jerry D. Hopkins

Evangelists
Dan Jenkins
Dean Reynolds
Jay Winter

Deacons
Joe Alcock
Ron Brackett
Stan Bronson
Pete Brown
Don Dodd
Mike Erickson
David Fenn
Dave Holaday
Jim Howell
Jeff Leslie
Dan McLeod
Carl Mack
Joseph Maloney
Chuck Milton
Greg Morris
Jerry Pittman
Bill Powell
Jim Rogers
David Sproule
Scott Studer
Russell Waggoner
Jim Whitesides

— 1989 —

Baptized (23)

Jan. 15	Joey Alcock
Mar. 12	Sheila Danford
Apr. 16	Katy Whitesides
Apr. 22	Douglas Ulmer
Apr. 23	Victor Beckles
Apr. 25	Sara Crocker
Apr. 25	Kelly McGilvery
Apr. 28	Brian Palmer
June 30	Layne McGilvery
July 05	Alburn Blake
July 30	Michael Rulapaugh
Aug. 02	Jamie Howell
Aug. 06	Janelle Ware
Sep. 05	Pete Harker
Sep. 10	Jimmie Banks
Sep. 22	Shane Davey
Oct. 01	Richard Cole
Oct. 01	Andrea Simpson
Oct. 01	Turkessa Fernander
Oct. 11	Stephen Humphrey
Oct. 24	Patrick O'Neill
Oct. 28	Mitch Clark
Nov. 11	Daniel John

Identified (46)

Jan. 22	Bobby & Asha Lall Dass
Jan. 25	Wayne Hawkins
Jan. 29	Ira & Mary Dodd
Jan. 29	Ronnie Crocker
Mar. 12	Don Danford
Mar. 12	Cassie Villanueva
Mar. 26	Donna Davis
Apr. 02	Bill & Inell Ingram
Apr. 05	Loretta Holaday
Apr. 16	Bill & Ronda Ingram
Apr. 16	Bill Barns
Apr. 16	Lula Burgess
June 18	Ron, Carolyn & Kim Cullom
June 25	Teri Leu
July 02	Lucy Costa
July 02	Evelio Escarria
July 23	Alan Waggoner
July 23	Kasandra Moore
July 23	Dessie Babacar & Crystol Mitchell
July 30	Greg Lovell
Aug. 06	Klee Hix
Aug. 20	Steve Glasgow
Aug. 20	Erik & Larah Erickson
Sep. 10	Robert & Jackie Price
Sep. 10	Cindy & Sheila Roberts
Sep. 13	Roger & Wendy Doyle
Sep. 17	Dan & Betsy Burden
Oct. 08	Marie Rogers
Oct. 15	Jamie Spearman
Nov. 19	Mike & Renee Barrios
Nov. 19	Ed & Ella Archer
Dec. 31	Barth Williams

— 1989 —

Restored (10)
Jan. 08   Lynn Blaisdell (Massey)
Jan. 29   Lonnie Smith
Apr. 16   Gerald J. Smith
July 23   Carrie Williams
Aug. 27   Carol Anstis
Sep. 24   Don & Marilee Boyd
Oct. 01   Dennis Utt
Dec. 03   John Belden
Dec. 17   Johnny Mark Davis

Births (9)
Feb. 21   Jamie Marie Sargies
Mar. 07   Justin Aaron Maloney
Mar. 30   Jake Tanner Rambold
Apr. 19   Katie Marie Wagner
Apr. 23   Bevin Bernard Edwards
Aug. 10   Nicole Elaine Joy
Sep. 08   Sean Ryan Keathley
Nov. 24   Jesse Manis
Dec. 03   Stacy Ann Hall

Weddings (6)
Mar. 25   Ephriam & Donna Davis
Apr. 22   Jody & Lynn Massey
July 15   Chip & Donna Stroh
Aug. 17   Alburn & Deborah Blake
Aug. 19   David & Rachael Lawrence
Sep. 23   Pete & Kristi Harker

Total Additions: 79   **287 Families; 496 Members**

— 1989 —

Died (6)
Jan. 24 Frank Wayne Ward
May 27 Marie Irvine
July 22 Voncile Kern
Aug. 07 Viola Whitacre
Nov. 02 Ada Belle Hopkins
Nov. 29 Ina Presnell

Moved Away (25)
Jan. 11 Randy Reese
Feb. 19 Wayne Hawkins
June 18 Don & Wanda Norwood
July 02 Cheryl Middleton
July 02 Louise, Shelley & Jimmy Hanna
July 02 Stephanie Pervola
July 02 Thelma Miller
July 13 John Dallas
July 16 Victor & Sydney Banuélos
July 17 Connie Sproule
Aug. 01 Jim & Mary Moores
Oct. 29 Jamie Spearman
Nov. 01 Kathleen Hane
Nov. 08 Evelio Escarria
Nov. 12 Becky Clement
Dec. 03 Patrick O'Neill
Dec. 06 Abby Murrell
Dec. 17 Daniel John
Dec. 17 Carl & Ann Henderson

Moved Membership (11)
Jan. 29 Lara Prairie
June 11 Bill Barns
Aug. 13 Jesse & Virginia Ford
Oct. 03 Erik & Larah Erickson
Oct. 03 Wiley Price
Nov. 05 Tommy Mathews
Nov. 08 Lillie Hill
Dec. 17 Ronnie Crocker
Dec. 17 Douglas Ulmer

Total Losses: 73   **287 Families; 496 Members**

— 1990 —

A Newcomers' Banquet was held on January 26 for all members since January 1989.

Ron Brackett became our Youth Director and church employee in January.

The theme for the annual Sweetheart Banquet hosted by the teens for the older members was the "Fabulous 50's" and was held on February 10.

February 25 was Bible Day, when members were shown various Bibles and study helps, and they were able to order them at cost.

A choral group from Hamilton, Alabama sang for us following evening services on March 11.

Our spring Gospel Meeting was conducted on March 18-22 with Tom Holland as the speaker.

Gerry Nix, Jeanie Langford's mother, was the speaker for the Eighth Annual Ladies' Day dinner on April 19.

Jim Rogers resigned as deacon on April 8.

The annual Junior/Senior Banquet was on April 20. David Jaress was selected first runner-up to the King.

The annual Road Rally was on May 5.

June 10 was designated as Bring-a-Friend Day. Following morning services, we had a picnic a Dreher Park.

Jay Winter moved to Goshen, Indiana on July 1.

Twelve of our young men conducted the evening services on August 26.

Seven new deacons were appointed on October 14. They were Tom Brown, Ron Cullom, John Hoelzer, Bill Ingram, Bill Ingram, Jr., Kevin Keathley, and Dirk Summerlot.

Spiritual Enrichment Weekend was on October 19-21 at the Lion's Club in Lake Wales.

Bill & Inell Ingram again invited everyone to their home for Thanksgiving dinner.

David Holaday resigned as deacon on December 2.

An adult holiday dinner was enjoyed by many at the Margarita y Amigas Restaurant, and then a period of fellowship and singing was held at the home of David & Bette Sproule.

— 1990 —

Elders
Johnny B. Davis
Don R. Hickerson
Joe D. Holland
Jerry D. Hopkins

Evangelists
Dan Jenkins
Dean Reynolds
Ron Brackett

Deacons
Joe Alcock
Pete Brown
Tom Brown
Ron Cullom
Don Dodd
Mike Erickson
David Fenn
John Hoelzer
Jim Howell
Bill Ingram, Sr.
Bill Ingram, Jr.
Kevin Keathley
Jeff Leslie
Dan McLeod
Carl Mack
Joseph Maloney
Chuck Milton
Greg Morris
Jerry Pittman
Bill Powell
David Sproule
Scott Studer
Dirk Summerlot
Russell Waggoner
Jim Whitesides

— 1990 —

Baptized (25)
Jan. 28 Michael Wells
Feb. 01 Robin Yates
Mar. 04 Ryan Brackett
Mar. 04 David Jaress
Mar. 11 Chris Dawson
Mar. 20 Robert Twining, Jr.
Mar. 20 Ernest L'Heureux
Mar. 21 Harry Schmidt
July 29 Shelly Roberts
Aug. 05 Jennifer Maloney
Aug. 12 Christopher Whitesides
Aug. 19 Roy Crocker, Sr.
Sep. 09 Rashon Medlock
Sep. 09 David McLeod
Sep. 16 Giselle Thomas
Oct. 07 Ron Weeks
Oct. 14 Marion Cummings
Nov. 11 Robert Tooker
Nov. 18 Ralph Raines
Nov. 18 Lucenia Reed
Nov. 18 Lonnie Williams
Nov. 18 Lee Sherrod
Nov. 28 Sarah Roberts
Dec. 16 Tamika Reed
Dec. 26 Cathy Sproule

Identified (15)
Feb. 18 Ron & Laverna Cullom
Feb. 25 Thelma Miller
Mar. 11 Shannon Ruano
Mar. 25 Rob & Beverly Stroud
Apr. 15 David & Cathy Payne
Apr. 22 Del & Helen Rataiczak
May 27 Danny & Jacqui Jenkins
July 22 Lila Clapp
Sep. 09 Dawn Zoller
Nov. 04 Violet Burke

Restored (8)
Mar. 22 Carl Miller
July 15 Wayne & Margie Fortenberry
Nov. 04 Maria Hackshaw
July 08 Richard McMasters
Aug. 15 H.R. Smith
Oct. 14 Brad Collier
Oct. 24 Peg MacDougal

Births (10)
Jan. 16 Tivoli Lark Lanham
Jan. 29 Brittany Nicole Massey
Mar. 06 Jessica Lauren Fox
Mar. 16 Eric Michael Minchey
Mar. 22 Jonathan David Harker
May 06 Rachel Anne Fuller
May 12 Christopher Allen Mitchell
Aug. 09 Dallas Pierre Williams
Aug. 11 Andrean Christine Blake
Oct. 01 Brittany Eloise Reeves

Weddings (4)
Mar. 03 Chuck & Robin Reeves
Mar. 20 Gerald & Pam Smith
July 28 David & Skye Brown
Dec. 29 Ricky & Sarah Smedley

Total Additions: 48

— 1990 —

Died (5)
Jan. 04 Gladys Daniel
Feb. 11 Herman Moody
Feb. 12 Minnie Piper
Mar. 18 Dennis Utt
Apr. 18 Lois Lail

Moved Away (42)
Feb. 14 Lottie Suddreth
Feb. 14 Cassie Villanueva
Feb. 25 Earl & Betty Wedge
Feb. 25 Tom & Betty Esmon
Feb. 25 Bernard & Donna Card
Mar. 25 Regina Aldridge
Apr. 04 Daryl Gordon
Apr. 18 Kevin & Diane Joy
May 26   Chet & Brenda Brown
May 26   Mark & Debbie Ware
May 26   Steve Glasgow
June 10 Pete & Kristi Harker
June 17 Janna Thompson
June 17 Eugene & Pam Edwards
June 23 Cindy Hanna
June 23 Jay & Betty Winter
June 29 Keith & Susan Joy
July 15 Andrew & Ande Fox
Aug. 01 Lane & Molly Johnson
Sep. 25 Polly Carpenter
Sep. 25 Ed Ohlenkamp
Sep. 30 Norma Ealy
Oct. 03 Denise Edwards
Nov. 25 Jody & Lynn Massey
Dec. 22 Gerald & Pam Smith
Dec. 22 Robyn, Robert & Rashon Medlock

Moved Membership (15)
Jan. 17 Lucy Costa
Mar. 14 Rachael Lawrence
Mar. 18 Vandine Montgomery
June 10 David Lawrence
June 13 Alf Reeder
Sep. 23 Jim Rogers Family (4)
Oct. 07 Chris & Paul Kachouroff
Oct. 21 John & Marguerite Kachouroff
Oct. 28 Jim & Laura Boone

Total Losses: 76   **274 Families; 473 Members**

— 1991 —

A series of classes for song leaders began on January 13 and continued for a month.

Tom Brown, one of our deacons, moved to Middleburg, Florida on January 23.

The Newcomers Banquet to honor all who became members at Palm Beach Lakes during the past year was conducted on Friday, January 25.

The theme for the Sweetheart Banquet for the Pioneers on Saturday, February 16 was "The Wild, Wild West."

Our spring meeting was conducted on March 3-7 with Bert Thompson as the speaker. Our day services were held at noon with sandwiches served for lunch.

Inell Ingram and Judie Jenkins spoke at the Ninth Annual Ladies' Day on Thursday, April 18. The theme this year was "Apples of Gold."

The annual Road Rally was held on Saturday, April 20.

Cordell Holloway of Dalton, Georgia and Joey Spann of Nashville, Tennessee were the speakers at the Teacher Training Workshop held on Friday Saturday, April 26-27.

A Ladies' Appreciation Breakfast served by the men of the congregation was held on Saturday, May 11.

At the annual Junior/Senior Banquet on May 17, Joey Alcock was selected King and Kristen Collier was chosen Queen. Joey's theme, "Coming Out of the Dark," was awarded the trophy for best theme.

A Family Seminar was conducted on May 24-26 with topics on "The Christian Home," with Bruce White of Guntersville, Alabama as the speaker.

A Teachers' Banquet was held on June 15.

In July, this congregation participated with the One Nation Under God project and had over two hundred lessons sent out.

Stan Bronson was ordained as an elder and Mike Barrios was appointed as a deacon on Sunday, July 7.

Ron Brackett directed the week of July 21-27 at the Central Florida Bible Camp.

A dinner to honor the widows of the congregation was held on Saturday, September 14.

We had 361 (the largest number for the year) present for Bible study on October 27 after a concerted effort to have everyone in Bible classes.

The Spiritual Enrichment Weekend was held on November 1-3 at the

— 1991 —

Lion's Club in Lake Wales.

The elders and deacons spent all day on Sunday, November 17 in an extensive planning session for things to be accomplished in 1992.

Bill & Inell Ingram again invited everyone who had no family in town to join them for Thanksgiving dinner.

The annual New Year's Eve Gathering was held following Bible classes on Tuesday, December 31.

Elders
Stan Bronson
Johnny B. Davis
Don R. Hickerson
Joe D. Holland
Jerry D. Hopkins

Evangelists
Dan Jenkins
Dean Reynolds
Ron Brackett

Deacons
Joe Alcock
Mike Barrios
Pete Brown
Ron Cullom
Don Dodd
Mike Erickson
David Fenn
John Hoelzer
Jim Howell
Bill Ingram, Sr.
Bill Ingram, Jr.
Kevin Keathley
Jeff Leslie
Dan McLeod
Carl Mack
Joseph Maloney
Chuck Milton
Greg Morris
Jerry Pittman
Bill Powell
David Sproule
Scott Studer
Dirk Summerlot
Russell Waggoner
Jim Whitesides

— 1991 —

Baptized (19)
Jan. 16 Valerie MacDougal
Feb. 27 Matthew Temple
Mar. 07 Joel McLeod
Apr. 03 Irene Carver
Apr. 17 Jordan Beasley
Apr. 28 Teri Taylor
May 12 Deborah Reed
June 17 Amy Affron
June 28 Christin Feeney
Aug. 04 Corinn Cox
Aug. 23 Bethany Heath
Sep. 11 Allison Price
Oct. 06 Matthew King
Oct. 27 Brian & Robin Swisher
Oct. 27 Beau Nelson
Oct. 30 Christina Colage
Dec. 18 Christopher Erickson
Dec. 31 Nadia King

Births (5)
Feb. 23 Timothy James Hoelzer
May 24 Brooke Ashlyn Rambold
May 24 William Daniel Jenkins
June 12 Lois DeAnn Davis
Aug. 17 Mark Allen Alford, Jr.

Weddings (4)
Feb. 23 Harold Pack & June Haines
Apr. 27 Jordan & Marshal Beasley
June 02 Charlie & Diane Cole Sharpe
Sep. 28 Doug & Lisa Lambert

Identified (38)
Jan. 20 David, Carolyn, Shane & Lauren Perkins
Feb. 10 Harold Pack
Feb. 10 Kirk Pogue
Feb. 10 Jimmie Lee Ciliberto
Mar. 27 Mark & Leslie Alford
Mar. 31 Blair & Lynette Brooker
Mar. 31 James Santos
Apr. 07 David & Rachael Lawrence
Apr. 10 David Garling
May 12 Lynn & Diane Heath, Timothy & Jeffrey
June 09 Jeff & Sharon Feeney
July 28 Johnny & Natasha Lawrence
Aug. 11 Larry & Kay Stallwood & Dawn
Aug. 18 Lisa Beverly
Sep. 04 Robert & Jean Conklin
Oct. 09 Jonathan & Julie Jenkins
Oct. 20 Jody & Lynn Massey
Oct. 27 Mylon & Paula Fulford
Oct. 27 Kathy DuBois
Dec. 08 Joyce Marshall
Dec. 08 Ed Ohlenkamp

Restored (3)
Apr. 17 Owen & Deidra Miley
Nov. 20 Chris Dawson

Total Additions: 60

— 1991 —

Died (4)
Mar. 15 Bill Coleman
Mar. 29 Elizabeth Cantrell
Apr. 03 Bill Morris
Sep. 01 J.W. Hagans

Moved Away (25)
Jan. 23 Tom & Linda Brown
         & Ashanti
Jan. 23 Teri Leu
Apr. 28 Kathy DuBois
May 26 Lisa Martin
June 28 Kerry & Linda Keathley
July 13 Al & Lisa Crandall & Greg
July 17 Carl Miller
July 28 Richard McMasters
Aug. 07 Don & Ruby Deel & Barbara
Aug. 25 Ulysses & Hattie Upshaw
Sep. 09 Clint McKee
Sep. 30 Craig & LaJuana Lanham
Oct. 20 Deborah Reed
Nov. 06 Courtney Carmack
Dec. 29 Janet Weil
Dec. 29 Dorothy Ridling

Moved Membership (8)
Jan. 02 Lula Hill
Jan. 23 Trina Wright
June 02 Wiley Price
June 02 Del & Helen Ratiaczak
Oct. 24 Shannon Ruano
Oct. 27 Tom & Rose Martens

Total Losses: 59　　　　　**263 Families; 468 Members**

— 1992 —

The annual Newcomers' Banquet was held on January 24 hosted by Area 3.

Ron Brackett began publishing a monthly Youth Alive Newsletter in January.

Our annual Sweetheart Banquet honoring the Pioneers and hosted by the teens was held on February 15. The theme was "Pirates."

Our spring Gospel Meeting was conducted on March 1-5 with Jerry Moffitt from Portland, Texas as the speaker.

Joe Alcock resigned as deacon on March 15.

On Sunday evening, March 29, the young men of the congregation directed the entire worship service with talks from Aaron Bronson and David Sproule, II.

In April, the ladies changed the format for their Bible classes. They will alternate Monday evenings with Thursday mornings with different speakers. They will be called the Helping Hands and will begin this schedule in May.

The speaker for the Tenth Annual Ladies' Day held on April 17 was Jane Foster of Birmingham, Alabama. The theme was "Because He Lives, I Can Face Tomorrow."

The "Announcement of a Dream" was announced on Sunday, May 3 with information from the elders on plans to build on the new property on Leo Lane. We also had dinner together after morning services.

A Singing Emphasis Weekend was conducted on May 8-10 by Gary Friedly of the Suncoast congregation.

A two-day retreat for the wives of church leaders (elders, deacons and preachers) was held on May 15-16 at the home of Inell Ingram.

At the annual Junior/Senior Banquet for South Florida on May 29, Aaron Bronson was selected first runner-up to the King.

The Teachers' Appreciation Banquet was held on May 29 honoring everyone who had taught Bible classes during the past year.

Bill Nicks was our guest speaker on June 7 in Dan's absence.

Ronnie Crocker spoke on drug abuse during the morning classes and preached for us during the morning worship period on Sunday, June 21.

Our week for the Central Florida Bible Camp conducted by Ron Brackett was July 19-25.

Hurricane Andrew struck South Florida, especially Homestead and Goulds, the first week in September. This congregation became very active in

— 1992 —

helping with aid for food and water early after it hit and channeled funds and food for several weeks following.

A very special workshop was conducted by Alan Highers of Henderson, Tennessee on October 8-11 including "Problems Facing the Church." He also spoke on "Why Are There So Many Churches?" and "If There Is Only One Church, How Can I Find It?"

A party for the Pioneers was given by the Junior High group on Saturday, October 17 with emphasis on World War II.

Bring-A-Friend Day was held on Sunday, November 8. We also had dinner together following morning services.

Spiritual Enrichment Weekend was held on November 13-15 at the Lion's Club in Lake Wales.

We began having a fifteen-minute Questions & Answers program on radio station WCNO in Stuart in November at 11:00 a.m. on the third Friday of each month.

The elders, deacons and preachers all-day workshop was held on Sunday, November 22.

Bill & Inell Ingram again invited everyone who had no family locally to share Thanksgiving Dinner and singing with them.

Bible study was changed to Thursday for December 31 only, so everyone could stay for the annual New Year's Eve gathering.

Elders	Deacons	Deacons (cont.)
Stan Bronson	Mike Barrios	Dan McLeod
Johnny B. Davis	Pete Brown	Carl Mack
Don R. Hickerson	Ron Cullom	Joseph Maloney
Joe D. Holland	Don Dodd	Chuck Milton
Jerry C. Hopkins	Mike Erickson	Greg Morris
	David Fenn	Jerry Pittman
Evangelists	John Hoelzer	Bill Powell
Dan Jenkins	Jim Howell	David Sproule
Dean Reynolds	Bill Ingram, Jr.	Scott Studer
Ron Brackett	Bill Ingram, Sr.	Dirk Summerlot
	Kevin Keathley	Russell Waggoner
	Jeff Leslie	Jim Whitesides

— 1992 —

Baptized (15)

Jan. 18	Rhonda Martinez
Jan. 20	Kari Ann Reeves
Jan. 20	Joan Nicastro
Feb. 02	Jason Johnson
Apr. 01	Marlene Cantu
May 28	Bevon Findley
July 19	Mrs. Edna Taylor
July 29	Bob & Heather Hilterman
Aug. 09	Shannon Stroh
Aug. 30	Loretta James
Oct. 14	Nikki Grilliot
Oct. 18	David Palmer, Jr.
Dec. 06	Evetta Collins
Dec. 09	Amberdenise Puckett

Births (7)

Feb. 10	Shea Chandler Brown
Mar. 03	Benjamin Craig Fulford
Apr. 25	Nicholas Albert Palmer
May 02	Emily Ann Keathley
Aug. 01	Andrew Clayton Jenkins
Sep. 07	Daniel Scott Wagner
Nov. 11	Ayanna Njeri Young

Weddings (2)

Jan. 04	Chris Kachouroff & Susan Alcock
June 13	Tim Cox & Susie Thomas

Identified (29)

Jan. 12	Chris Kachouroff
Jan. 19	Walter & Penny Hahn
Feb. 09	Sue Bowland
Apr. 01	Sybil Small
Apr. 19	Philip & Mary Porter
Apr. 26	Ralph & Ady Romero, Sr.
May 10	Mrs. Wm. Uppie Mercer
May 10	Miss Edna Milsap
July 05	Miss Kelly Shepard
July 19	Joe Miller
July 29	Mrs. Joan Hilterman
Aug. 05	Brent Clark
Aug. 16	Derrick & Patsy Sikes
Aug. 19	John Thomas
Aug. 23	Hattie Upshaw
Aug. 30	Mrs. Emily McCauley
Sep. 13	Mrs. Lola Walker-Edwards
Sep. 27	Kasandra Moore
Sep. 27	Christopher Mitchell
Oct. 04	Aren Elizee
Nov. 08	Matthew Jones
Nov. 18	John & Myra Ashburn
Nov. 29	Dorothy Wilson
Dec. 20	Deborah Reed

Total Additions: 44

— 1992 —

Died (5)
Mar. 29 Hank Flowers
Apr. 09 Lula Burgess
May 03 Mary Dodd
June 10 Garold Van Helten
Nov. 10 Richard Cole

Moved Away (24)
Jan. 22 Charles Massey
Feb. 02 Natasha Lawrence
Apr. 08 Belle Moody
Apr. 21 Rhonda Martinez
May 17 Doug Carmack
May 17 Kitty Stone
May 17 Lisa Beverly
June 19 Annette Sproule
June 19 David, Carol, William & Janice Wedge
July 24 David, Carolyn, Shane & Lauren Perkins
Aug. 06 Dawn Stallwood
Aug. 14 Jonathan & Julie Jenkins
Aug. 31 Rob & Beverly Stroud
Oct. 28 Barth Williams
Oct. 28 Joe & Thelma Miller

Moved Membership (6)
Jan. 05 John Belden
Jan. 12 Rachael Lawrence
Mar. 01 Pat Gonzales
Mar. 29 Don & Cathy Seay
Nov. 15 Edna Milsap

Total Losses: 45   **274 Families; 467 Members**

— 1993 —

Dan Jenkins began using items from "25 Years Ago" in the bulletin in January.

The Newcomers' Banquet for all who became members during the last year was hosted by Area 4 on January 29.

Training for Living Classes were conducted on Sunday evening, January 31 with Tommy Pauldo, Don Hickerson and Jerry & Shirley Hopkins teaching.

Dan Jenkins conducted a two-month Sunday morning class on Marriage, Divorce and Remarriage in February and March.

The annual Sweetheart Banquet provided by the teens for the Pioneers was held on February 13. The theme was "Hurrah for Hollywood."

Our spring meeting was conducted on March 7-11 with James Meadows as the speaker.

Three new deacons were appointed on Sunday, April 4: Jeff Feeney, Dan Fuller and Harold Pack.

The Eleventh Annual Ladies' Day was held on April 8 with Debi Ingram Watson from Texarkana, Arkansas as the speaker. Debi is the daughter of Bill & Inell Ingram.

On May 2, the "Dream Team" presented plans and hopes of the new building to the congregation. Cans were distributed to be filled with money to be added to the building fund.

A class for young preachers by Dan Jenkins was started on May 9 for two months.

The theme of the annual Junior/Senior Banquet held on May 14 was "A Whole New World." Jamie Howell was selected first runner-up to the Queen, Brandon Whitesides was selected second runner-up to the King, Scotty Studer as first runner-up to the King, and David Sproule II was selected King.

Following a study on Stewardship for one quarter, V.P. Black spoke to us four times on Sunday, May 23, on how to improve our giving.

Ronnie Crocker graduated from Memphis School of Preaching on June 20 and began working with the Jupiter congregation in a prison ministry.

On June 27, many of our members brought "brown bag" lunches and ate together following morning services. They donated what would have been spent if we ate out to the building fund.

Ron Brackett directed the week of July 25-31 at the Central Florida Bible Camp in Eustis, Florida.

— 1993 —

"Bring-a-Friend Day" was held on August 22 followed by dinner on the grounds.

Susan Rawls, a new member from Tallahassee, began classes on Sunday evenings at 5:30 p.m. for all who would like to learn sign language.

The annual Teachers' Appreciation Banquet was prepared for all who taught during the past year on Sunday, August 29.

A retreat for the wives of elders, deacons and preachers was held on October 8-9 at the home of Inell Ingram.

The Junior High youth hosted a costume party for the Pioneers on October 9.

We had special services on October 17 with morning services followed by dinner on the grounds, then evening services at 1:00 p.m.

Training for Living classes on October 31 were taught by Everett Chambers, Ron W. Cullom, Ephriam Davis and Jim Howell.

Our regular hours of worship were changed in November. Sunday evening was changed from 6:30 p.m. to 6:00 p.m., and Wednesday evening was changed from 7:30 p.m. to 7:00 p.m.

Thanksgiving dinner was prepared at the Ingram's again for all who wanted to attend followed by a period of singing.

The elders, deacons and preachers had an all-day planning session on Sunday, December 12.

One of our deacons, Chuck Milton, placed membership at Jupiter.

Elders	**Deacons**	
Stan Bronson	Mike Barrios	Jeff Leslie
Johnny Davis	Pete Brown	Dan McLeod
Don Hickerson	Ron Cullom	Carl Mack
Joe Holland	Don Dodd	Joe Maloney
Jerry Hopkins	Mike Erickson	Greg Morris
	Jeff Feeney	Harold Pack
Evangelists	David Fenn	Jerry Pittman
Dan Jenkins	Dan Fuller	Bill Powell
Dean Reynolds	John Hoelzer	David Sproule
Ron Brackett	Jim Howell	Scott Studer
	Bill Ingram, Sr.	Dirk Summerlot
	Bill Ingram, Jr.	Russell Waggoner
		Jim Whitesides

— 1993 —

Baptized (11)
Feb. 17 Manuel Ortiz
Feb. 22 Roy McDowell
Mar. 03 John Schuler
Mar. 09 Keith Adams
Apr. 18 Marty Williams
May 27 Hannah Garcia
Aug. 18 Leon Johnson
Sep. 22 Bari Bliss
Oct. 17 Anne Rollyford
Oct. 31 Jody Francis
Nov. 21 Willette Curry

Identified (25)
Jan. 10 Tilden Hedley
Jan. 24 Wiley Price
Feb. 21 George Hackshaw
Mar. 09 Ramona Andrews
Apr. 04 Kym Spurlock
Apr. 04 Pamela Stringer
May 02 Steve Mitchell
May 30 Don & Pam Williams
June 06 Tim Nettleton
June 06 Joe Wells
June 06 Everett Chambers
July 18 Pearl Blount
Aug. 15 Susan Rawls
Sep. 19 David Thompson
Sep. 29 Jean-Claude Previlus
Oct. 03 Paul, Bev, Omar & Tahneece Houdyshelt
Oct. 10 Lucy Costa
Oct. 10 Woodie & Boots Wood
Oct. 17 Bill & Michelle Kay

Restored (2)
Nov. 07 Andrea Simpson Milton
Dec. 01 James Smith

Births (7)
Jan. 22 Alexandria Naomi Alford
Mar. 02 Thomas Dean Genduso
Mar.   Jacob Thomas Menendez
Mar. 29 Katie Elizabeth Hahn
Apr. 22 Jeremy Adam Maloney
May 20 Charles Austin Reeves
Aug. 14 David Blair Brooker

Weddings (6)
Jan. 09 Matthew Jones & Kasandra Moore
Jan. 19 Matthew Temple & Nikki Grilliot
July 03 Dan Mefford & Dawn Stallwood
July 10 Buck Buchanan & Kym Spurlock
July 17 Tim Nettleton & Hannah Garcia
Oct. 02 John Gaessler & Annette Sproule

Died (8)
Jan. 08 Della Burleson
Feb. 11 Billy Crocker
Mar. 09 Tom Massey
Apr. 28 Fred Duerr
May 27 Klee Hix
June 29 Marshall Bourland
Aug. 19 Ruth Burgess
Dec. 12 John Jackson

Total Additions: 38

— 1993 —

Moved Away (26)

Jan. 02   Don & Jean Spurlock
Mar. 17   John Schuler
Apr. 11   Tilden Headley
Apr. 21   Doug & Steven Carmack
June 08   Bob & Jean Conklin
June 25   Matthew & Nikki Temple
July 06   Ed Ohlenkamp
Aug. 01   Bobby & Asha Lall Dass
Aug. 01   Walter & Penny Hahn
Aug. 04   Keith Adams
Aug. 08   Joe Wells
Aug. 22   Mae Pierce
Aug. 22   Bevon Findley
Aug. 22   Deborah Reed
Aug. 29   Kirk Pogue
Aug. 29   Kelly Shepard
Sep. 05   Josephine Plumlee
Sep. 22   Johnny Lawrence
Oct. 31   Faye Wilson
Dec. 28   Dawn Dodd

Moved Membership (14)

Mar. 03   Robert Walker, Jr.
Mar. 07   Uppie Mercer
Apr. 11   Dawn Z. Oller
May 18   Steve Mitchell
July 18   Roy & Sara Crocker
Aug. 01   Maria Hackshaw
Aug. 04   Maureen Machan
Aug. 11   Loretta Holaday
Aug. 11   Angellia Twiggs
Sep. 29   Larry & Kay Stallwood
Dec. 26   Chuck & Debbie Milton

Total Losses: 84   **249 Families; 412 Members**

— 1994 —

We had a workshop on personal work on January 29 with Don Jones as the teacher entitled "Serving More in '94."

The Newcomers' Banquet for all who became members during last year was hosted by Area 1 on February 4.

One of our deacons, Jim Whitesides, moved away on February 20.

Our spring meeting was held on March 6-9 with Wendell Winkler as the speaker.

A new visitation program began on March 6. Harold Pack was chairman of the committee. New visitation packets were designed and were very well-received by those visited. A new Area Program began on March 12 with twelve areas replacing the former four areas.

The annual Sweetheart Banquet provided by the teens for the Pioneers was held on February 12.

The Twelfth Annual Ladies' Day was held on April 21. Elsie Huffard, a teacher at Freed-Hardeman University, was the speaker. The topic was "Back to Basics."

The Pioneers went on a boat cruise and luncheon on April 12. There was a congregational corn roast at the park on Lighthouse Drive on April 30.

At the annual Junior/Senior Banquet held on May 6, Sheila Roberts was selected second runner-up to the Queen and Becky Brackett was selected Queen.

We had a Bible Bowl on May 7 for students in grades 3-12 on the "Gospel of Mark."

One of our deacons, Mike Barrios, moved away on June 6.

David Sproule worked with the teens for the summer.

The Central Florida Bible Camp week directed by Ron Brackett was held on July 24-30.

Jacqui Jenkins & Peggy Hall began a new class on "Communicating with the Deaf" on August 26.

Mary Sproule resigned as custodian of the church building effective July 1. David & Bette Sproule agreed to continue these duties until the first of the year.

There was a two-day Ladies' Retreat at the Holiday Inn on Singer Island. The theme was "Love for One Another." About fifty of our ladies attended.

— 1994 —

The annual Teachers' Appreciation Banquet was on August 28.

Robert, Mary and Maria Martin, missionaries in the Pacific who we help to support, visited with us on August 14-16. Robert spoke to us on Sunday, August 16.

Dr. Bert Thompson conducted another Creation/Evolution Seminar on October 28-30.

Three new deacons were appointed on December 4: David Brown, Ephriam Davis and Phil Porter.

The elders, deacons and preachers had an all-day planning session on Sunday, November 13.

Our teens competed in a Bible Bowl for students in grades 3-12 at the Jupiter/Tequesta congregation on November 19 and one group won a trophy.

The regular New Years Eve Gathering was held on Saturday, December 31.

Elders	Deacons	Deacons (cont.)
Stan Bronson	David Brown	Jeff Leslie
Johnny Davis	Pete Brown	Dan McLeod
Don Hickerson	Ron Cullom	Carl Mack
Joe Holland	Ephriam Davis	Joe Maloney
Jerry Hopkins	Don Dodd	Greg Morris
	Mike Erickson	Harold Pack
Evangelists	Jeff Feeney	Jerry Pittman
Dan Jenkins	David Fenn	Phil Porter
Dean Reynolds	Dan Fuller	Bill Powell
Ron Brackett	John Hoelzer	David Sproule
	Jim Howell	Scott Studer
	Bill Ingram, Sr.	Dirk Summerlot
	Bill Ingram, Jr.	Russell Waggoner

— 1994 —

Baptized (27)

Jan. 30   Elizabeth Erickson
Apr. 17   Bill Reichel
Apr. 24   Elizabeth Franklin
May 01   Tasha Bridgett
May 08   Nakia Gilmore
May 15   Monica Carson
May 15   Jimmy Cunningham
May 22   Melinda Grimsley
May 29   Marcie Hladik
May 29   Samuel Quinn
June 09   Rachel Dodd
July 03   Icilda Hopkins
July 17   Henry Hucks
July 24   Marc Frederick
Aug. 07   Alissa Bronson
Aug. 24   Miriam & Ingrid Sainio
Oct. 16   Lovetta Harmon
Oct. 16   Alexandria Harmon
Oct. 23   Laura Leslie
Oct. 26   James Haymin
Nov. 07   Deborah Kutcher
Nov. 25   Shirley Haymin
Dec. 04   Jessica Menendez
Dec. 11   Linda Wright
Dec. 11   Caraline Wedges
Dec. 13   George Williamson, Jr.
Dec. 25   Heather Bullock
Dec. 25   Daniel Feeney

Identified (20)

Feb. 06   Margie Cunningham
Feb. 20   Argie Moore
Apr. 17   Norma Marchand
Apr. 24   David Dallsingh
May 15   Norman Curington
May 22   Donna Bleau
June 05   Tom & Rose Martens
July 17   Bobby & Asha Lall Dass
July 24   Valerie Sordiff
Aug. 07   Maxine Jacoby
Aug. 14   Harry, Mary & Stacy Reese
Aug. 14   Megan Cox
Aug. 21   Maria Hackshaw
Oct. 09   Jacqueline Creary
Nov. 13   Debbie Haymin
Nov. 13   John Dean

Restored (5)

Mar. 20   Joyce Green
Apr. 13   Silas Lynch
Apr. 20   Lonnie Williams
Nov. 27   Vanessa Nelson
Dec. 18   Morrius Bleau

— 1994 —

Weddings

Jan. 07	Willie Smith & Giselle Thomas
Feb. 08	Phillip Lamb & Sabrina Menendez
May	Lee Dell Hester & Senia Wade
May 21	Jerry Blazer & Martha
June 04	Jessee Gilley & Renee Fenn
June 30	Samuel Quinn & Mary Eutsey
Sep. 03	Bill Lockhart & Sandy Wiggins
Nov. 19	Buzz Nelson & Kathy DuBois

Births

Mar. 08	Lee Dell Hester, Jr.
Mar. 16	David Glenn Payne, II
Apr. 03	Jerome Milton, Jr.
May 09	MonteKia Gilmore Jones
Oct. 27	Andrew Lorenzo Bleau
Dec. 14	Kelly Angela Hall

Total Additions: 54   **242 Families; 405 Members**

— 1994 —

Died (7)
May 10 Nakia Gilmore
June 21 Grady Lee
July 18 Jody Francis
Oct. 03 Beatrice Brumfiel
Oct. 09 Ardell Hatfield
Oct. 30 Manny Ortiz
Nov. 09 Woodie Wood

Moved Away (29)
Feb. 02 Sue Bowland
Feb. 20 Jim Whitesides family (6)
Mar. 13 Mary Flowers
May 25 Mike & Nita Manis
June 06 Mike & Renee Barrios
June 08 Renee Fenn
June 26 Tim & Hannah Nettleton
Jul.. 20 Kym Buchanan
July 20 John Thomas
July 31 Susan Rawls
Aug. 10 Frances Walker
Aug. 14 Jimmy Cunningham
Sep. 11 Adam Crandall
Sep. 22 Priscilla Fussell
Oct. 16 Dorothy Wilson
Oct. 23 Penny Minchey
Oct. 23 Kenneth Dodd
Dec. 11 Everett Chambers
Dec. 11 Rudolph Gordon
Dec. 28 Phil & Jean Townsend

Moved Membership (13)
Jan. 01 Chuck & Debbie Milton
Feb. 02 George Hackshaw
Feb. 02 Susan & Chris Kachouroff
Mar. 03 Don & Marilee Boyd
Mar. 03 Patricia Copeland
May 22 Sheila Roberts
May 29 David Thompson
July 06 Lucy Costa
Nov. 01 David Dallsingh
Nov. 27 Norman Curington

Total Losses: 66   242 Families; 405 Members

— 1995 —

Training for Living classes were conducted on January 29 on the topics of "So You Wanna Be Rich," "Premillenialism," and "Situation Ethics."

The Newcomers' Banquet for all new members during the last year was hosted by Areas 4, 5 and 6 and was held on February 24.

A new Area program began on February 26 returning to four areas instead of twelve.

We had a day of fasting on March 8 in preparation for our upcoming Gospel Meeting. Our spring Gospel Meeting was conducted on March 12-16 by Tom Holland.

A drama group from Freed-Hardeman University (For Heaven's Sake) performed for the teens after services on Wednesday night, March 22.

The Young Adults had a corn roast in North Palm Beach on March 25.

New Testament tapes were made available for all who would listen together as a congregation beginning on April 17.

The Thirteenth Annual Ladies' Day was held on April 20 with Rose Coleman as the speaker. The theme was "Mirror, Mirror."

A Men's Retreat was held on April 21-22 at the Gold Coast Camp.

The Junior/Senior Banquet was held at the Fort Lauderdale Marina Marriot on April 21. Chris Fry was selected first runner-up to the King.

Training for Living classes were conducted on April 23. Subjects were "Every Joint Supplies," "Edifying One Another," "Motivating Others to Do Good Work," and "The Lottery."

During May, sermons were focused on the family.

The North Federal Church building was sold in April.

A Widow's Brunch was held on May 20 at the home of Dan & Judie Jenkins.

David Sproule worked with our teens during the summer.

New carpet was installed in the auditorium the week of June 4 by Buzz Nelson.

One of our deacons, David Fenn, moved away on June 27.

Our Thirty Year Homecoming (for thirty years on 36th Street) was on July 16. We had dinner on the grounds and a 1:00 p.m. service.

The week of July 23-29 was our week at the Central Florida Bible Camp this year. It was conducted by Ron Brackett.

This congregation conducted a South Florida Youth Rally on August

— 1995 —

11-13 with Bert Thompson of Montgomery, Alabama as the speaker. The theme was "Fortifying the Faith of Teens."

A Ladies' Retreat was held at the Embassy Suites Resort on Singer Island on September 22-23. The theme was "The Hand of God."

Training for Living Classes were conducted on August 27 with a Panel of Parents discussing problems with children, and classes on "Biblical Principles to Keep Marriages Alive," "Coping with Loneliness," and "A Review of Mormonism."

A Bible Bowl for teens was conducted here on September 16. Eleven congregations were invited and 285 attended.

Michael Hatcher was guest speaker on Sunday morning, October 15. Wayne Jackson conducted a seminar on Evidences on October 20-22.

Training for Living Classes were conducted on November 19. Subjects were "Rearing Adolescent Children," "Training Small Children in Worship," and "An Overview of Church History."

The elders, deacons & preachers conducted an all-day workshop on November 12.

Joe & Marian Holland opened their home on Thanksgiving for all who had no family in town.

Elders	Deacons	Deacons (cont.)
Stan Bronson	David Brown	Dan McLeod
Johnny Davis	Pete Brown	Carl Mack
Don Hickerson	Ron Cullom	Joseph Maloney
Joe Holland	Ephriam Davis	Greg Morris
Jerry Hopkins	Don Dodd	Harold Pack
	Mike Erickson	Jerry Pittman
Evangelists	Jeff Feeney	Phil Porter
Dan Jenkins	Dan Fuller	Bill Powell
Dean Reynolds	John Hoelzer	David Sproule
Ron Brackett	Jim Howell	Scott Studer
	Bill Ingram, Sr.	Dirk Summerlot
	Bill Ingram, Jr.	Russell Waggoner
	Jeff Leslie	

— 1995 —

Baptized (18)

Jan. 08 Joanne Sandeen
Jan. 08 Josephine Bass
Mar. 16 Tim Mahlbacher
Apr. 23 Lenoris Davis
May 28 Susie Cox
June 04 Cora Lee Daniels
June 04 Mattie Cox
June 11 Reginald Arnold
June 20 Dianna Girten
July 02 LaDawn Collier
July 02 Angelo Jenkins
July 09 Willie Cox
July 09 Tumeka Cox
Sep. 03 Rose Boyd
Sep. 03 Cliff Boyd
Oct. 17 Ethan Bronson
Dec. 10 Sean Saunders
Dec. 24 Diana Tek

Restored (10)

Jan. 01 Bobby & Cynthia Ingraham
Jan. 11 J.J. Johnson
June 04 Hodges I. Davis
June 11 Felicia Arnold
Dec. 06 Senia Hester
Dec. 10 Johnny & Blossom Young
Dec. 24 Elizabeth Bedminster
Dec. 31 Henry Bass

Identified (24)

Jan. 15 Jackie Stout
Feb. 19 Evelyn Gaston
Mar. 08 Rosemary Franklin
May 07 John & Melinda Daniels
June 18 John & Annette Gaessler
June 18 Todd Hunt
July 02 Art & Gina Tek,
         Garrison & Kathy
July 16 Bill & Lori Boyd
July 23 Corinn Cox
Aug. 06 Dan Garvin
Aug. 20 Ray Hughes
Aug. 27 Clara Bond
Sep. 17 Clarence, Gloria & Nickell Dixon
Oct. 01 Emily Hopkins
Oct. 15 Janette Grenier
Oct. 15 Henry Thomson

Weddings (2)

June 03 Darrell Young & Ingrid Sainio
June 09 Phil & Dianna Girten

Births (6)

Feb. 22 Jelani Dar Young
Apr. 07 Kristen Nicole & Lauren Ruth Fuller
June 16 Kimberly Denise Mitchell
Aug. 15 Megan Nicole Stroh
Nov. 23 Lavonte Hester
Dec. 13 Daniel Lorick Harmon

Total Additions: 52

— 1995 —

Moved Away (24)
Feb. 05 Tom & Neta Genduso
Feb. 22 Jean-Claude Previlus
Feb. 22 Joyce Green
Mar. 02 John Dean
June 19 Ira Dodd
June 19 Rachel Dodd
June 22 Marie Duerr
June 27 David & Shirley Fenn
July 23 Bobby, Asha, Vadin & Varisa Lall Dass
Aug. 07 Paul & Beverly Houdyshelt, Omar & Tahneece
Aug. 13 Marcie Hladik
Aug. 27 Olie Murr
Aug. 27 Garrison Strickland
Nov. 05 Norma Marchand
Dec. 20 Ruth Bruguiere
Dec. 31 Sandy Lockhart

Moved Membership (4)
Aug. 06 Bob & Juanetta Walker
Sep. 24 Harold & Genny Keathley

Total Losses: 45   **241 Families; 411 Members**

— 1996 —

Beginning January 21, we had a three-week training session series on Sunday afternoons to learn how to use the Jule Miller film strips.

The Newcomers' Banquet for all new members during last year was hosted by Area 1 on January 26.

Our spring meeting was conducted on March 3-7 by Garland Elkins from Memphis, Tennessee.

The congregation began to listen to the tapes of the Bible to "Read the Bible through Together" on March 3.

The elders, deacons, preachers and their wives had a Leadership Dinner together at Piccadilly Restaurant on March 29.

Don Hickerson resigned as elder on April 4. He was appointed in 1984 and served faithfully for twelve years.

Dan Jenkins began special classes in Greek and in-depth studies on Monday evenings on April 15. This continued for several months.

The Fourteenth Annual Ladies' Day was held on April 18 with Betty Davis, Shirley Hopkins and Gwen Lyons speaking on "Lessons I Have Learned from Children."

The Junior/Senior Banquet was held at the Radisson Suite Hotel in Palm Beach Gardens on May 17. Jennifer Maloney was selected Queen and Shane Studer was selected King.

A Widows' Brunch was held at the home of Judie Jenkins on May 18.

On May 19, we had dinner-on-the-ground at the new property following morning services.

David Sproule worked with our teens during the summer.

Nine teens and four adults traveled to Lynchburg, Virginia on July 5-13 to do community service work and to teach a Vacation Bible School. Bruce DeMoss was the preacher there.

The week of July 21-27 was our week at the Central Florida Bible Camp this year. It was conducted by Ron Brackett.

Ralph Gilmore was with us on August 9-10 for a Youth Rally. The theme was "The War Is On."

A Ladies' Retreat was held at the Embassy Suites Resort on Singer Island on September 6-7. Speakers were Judie & Jacqui Jenkins, Donna Davis and June Pack.

Spiritual Enrichment Weekend was started again on October 4-5 at Gold Coast Christian Camp in Lake Worth.

— 1996 —

John Hoelzer and Jeff Feeney resigned as deacons on October 13, and the names of Bill Boyd and Gary Jenkins were put before the congregation to be deacons. They were appointed on Sunday, October 27.

Our First South Florida Lectureship entitled "Guided By The Light" was conducted on November 8-10 with Ancil Jenkins (Sunset, Miami), Joe Roberts (Suncoast), Don Jones (Stuart), Gary Davenport (West Broward), Dan Jenkins (Palm Beach Lakes), Jack McGhee (Sebring), Gale Nelson (Coconut Grove, Miami), Joe Holland (Palm Beach Lakes), Bill Boyd (Palm Beach Lakes), Carolyn McWhorter (Lake Tarpon, Tarpon Springs), Gary Jenkins (Palm Beach Lakes), Stan Bronson & Ron Brackett (Palm Beach Lakes), Leon Green (Lake Street, Stuart), Gary Wyder (Lake Butler), Benny Santiago, Jr. (Dodd Road), Al Washington (WPB congregation), Boyd Williams (Vero Beach), Frank Parker (Sebring), Bill Ingram, Jr. & Jim Howell (Palm Beach Lakes), Ernest Mackifield (WPB congregation), Lawrence Gilmore (Westside), Jan Blackwell (West Broward), Ronnie Crocker (Jupiter), and Corey Glover (Hallandale) as speakers.

Every Member Present Day was on November 17. Purpose cards were handed out to the members in anticipation of the new building next year. The elders, deacons and preachers conducted an all-day workshop/planning session on this day.

Wednesday evening Bible study was changed to Tuesday, December 31, and our regular New Year's Eve party was held afterward.

Elders	**Deacons**	**Deacons (cont.)**
Stan Bronson	Bill Boyd	Dan McLeod
Johnny Davis	David Brown	Carl Mack
Joe Holland	Pete Brown	Joseph Maloney
Jerry Hopkins	Ron Cullom	Greg Morris
	Ephriam Davis	Harold Pack
Evangelists	Don Dodd	Jerry Pittman
Dan Jenkins	Mike Erickson	Phil Porter
Dean Reynolds	Dan Fuller	Bill Powell
Ron Brackett	Jim Howell	David Sproule
	Bill Ingram, Sr.	Scott Studer
	Bill Ingram, Jr.	Dirk Summerlot
	Gary Jenkins	Russell Waggoner
	Jeff Leslie	

— 1996 —

Baptized (16)
Jan. 14 Mandy Strickland
Feb. 11 Trey Ingram
Feb. 18 Jerome Milton
Feb. 25 Gladys Milton Cannon
Feb. 25 Amber Pittman
Mar. 03 Gladys Cleare
Mar. 03 DeAndre Harmon
Mar. 03 Tommie Kennedy
Mar. 03 Latoya Kennedy
Mar. 04 Richard Sineath
Mar. 04 Kelly Tek
Mar. 07 Kelly Affron
Mar. 31 Charles Sainio
July 21 Jeremiah Cummings
Sep. 15 Senyaon Coleman
Dec. 22 Tia Clemans

Weddings (6)
Jan. 24 Jim Courtright & Joanne Sandeen
May 18 Brent Clark & Yvonne Rogers
May 25 Aaron Bronson & Leah Fair
July 19 David Sproule, II & Traci Smith
Nov. 27 Jayly Jackson & Jennifer Maloney
Nov. 30 Kelvin Samuel & Gail Bedminster

Births (3)
Mar. 13 Rachel Victoria Payne
July 25 Grant Elton Fuller
Nov. 04 Chad Parker Brown

Identified (28)
Feb. 25 Norma Marchand
Mar. 17 Susan Freire
Apr. 07 Clarence & Brenda Cook
Apr. 28 Susan, Rob, Amanda & Brad Shelt
Apr. 28 Hardy & Rachel Cooper
Apr. 28 Bill & Joyce Bain
Apr. 28 Charles Norton
May 19 Ruby Hilton
May 26 Arthur Williams
May 26 Yvonne Clark
June 26 Theodorea Simmons
July 28 Traci Sproule
Sep. 01 John H. Coppens
Oct. 06 Glena Maggart & Scott
Oct. 16 Eileen Rogers
Oct. 20 Andrea Spradlin
Nov. 06 Merlene Stoker
Nov. 10 David & Carolyn Perkins
Dec. 08 Gail Bedminster Samuel
Dec. 29 Joyce Parker

Restored (4)
June 23 Ray Hughes
July 03 Willie Smith
July 21 Jim Cunningham
Sep. 29 Kenneth Long

Total Additions: 48

— 1996 —

Died (6)
Jan. 04　Ingrid Young
Jan. 06　Ruth Middleton
July 02　James Santos
Sep. 04　Isaac Burgess
Dec. 01　Mary Hood
Dec. 07　Manuel Pacheco

Moved Away (22)
Feb. 25　Elizabeth Bedminster
Apr. 07　Ralph & Ady Romero
Apr. 26　John Daniels
May 26　Charles Middleton
May 26　Elizabeth Franklin
June 23　Jamie Howell
June 23　Aaron Bronson
Aug. 25　Megan & Corinn Cox
Sep. 13　Reggie & Felicia Arnold
Sep. 22　Golden & Linda Beane
Sep. 22　Florence Bourland
Sep. 29　Pearl Blount
Oct. 17　Todd Hunt
Dec. 18　Glena & Scott Maggart
Dec. 22　Harry, Mary & Stacy Reese

Moved Membership (3)
Sep. 04　Hattie Upshaw
Dec. 15　Woody & Cyndi Guin

Total Losses: 32　　　　　　　**249 Families; 426 Members**

— 1997 —

Our annual Newcomers' Banquet for all new members during the last year was hosted by Area 2 on January 31 at the building.

The Seniors hosted the Sweetheart Banquet for the Pioneers on February 16.

There was a Men's Retreat at the Gold Coast Camp for all men of the congregation on February 21-22.

In March, students in Grades 3-5 put together a time capsule to be opened in ten years.

Our spring Gospel Meeting was conducted on March 2-6 with Richard Melson as the speaker.

The congregation honored Dan & Judie Jenkins for their fifteen years of service on April 13. A scrapbook with letters, notes and cards was presented to them.

Carolyn McWhorter, from Tarpen Springs, Florida, was the speaker for the Fifteenth Annual Ladies' Day on April 17. The theme was "The Beauty of Jesus. "

The annual Junior/Senior Banquet was held at the Don Shula Hotel & Golf Club in Miami on April 18.

New Testament tapes were made available for all who would like to listen together as a congregation beginning the first week in April.

David & Traci Sproule arrived in May to become part of our work here. He will be working primarily with the teens.

The annual Widows' Brunch was held on May 17 at the home of Judie Jenkins.

One of our deacons, Bill Powell, died on May 18.

Our week at the Central Florida Bible Camp conducted by Ron Brackett was July 20-26.

Dan Jenkins, Bill Boyd and David Sproule, II conducted a training class for young men of the congregation in grades 3-12. It began on July 13 and continued for several weeks.

On August 9, many of our young people and adults went to Lake Placid to help them with a door-knocking effort.

The theme for the annual Ladies' Retreat held on September 5-6 at the Palm Beach Gardens Marriott was "Where Are Your Treasures?" Speakers were Inell Ingram, Lori Boyd and Mary Brown.

Groundbreaking ceremonies were held for our new building on Leo

— 1997 —

Lane following morning worship on August 17. Many pictures were taken and everyone who wished brought a shovel to be a part of it.

We had "Bring-a-Friend Day" on September 21 with dinner on the grounds followed by evening worship at 1:00 p.m.

The men of the congregation held a Men's Retreat at the building all day on October 4.

The Second South Florida Lectureship, entitled "The Christian Home in a Secular Society" was conducted on November 7-9. Keynote speakers were Dan Jenkins (Palm Beach Lakes); Gary Davenport (West Broward); David Shanks (Overton, Miami); Boyd Williams (Vero Beach); and Ernest Mackifield (Third Street). Song leaders were Jerry Hopkins (Palm Beach Lakes); Larry Porter (Jupiter/Tequesta); George Barber (West Broward); Dan Jenkins (PBL); and Wes Holland (PBL). Teaching classes were Clifford Reel (Lake Placid); Gerry Nicks (Jupiter/Tequesta); Joe Roberts (Suncoast); David Sproule II (PBL); Dane Waggoner (High Point, NC); John Hoelzer (PBL); Ancil Jenkins (Sunset, Miami); Ron Brackett (PBL); Jim Howell (PBL); Chris Mitchell (PBL); Joe Wild (Vero Beach); Jerry Hopkins (PBL); Cindy Roberts (PBL); Gale Nelson (Coconut Grove, Miami); Milton Irvin (Suncoast); Al Washington (Third Street); Gary Jenkins (PBL); James Haymin (PBL); Bill Nicks (Trinidad); Bill Boyd (PBL); Leon Green (Stuart); Lawrence Gilmore (Westside); Ronnie Crocker (Jupiter/Tequesta); and Benny Santiago (Dodd Road). In addition, there was a panel of elders from Palm Beach Lakes and Jupiter/Tequesta for a Questions & Answers session. The lectureship was well supported by other congregations in the area.

On November 16, the elders, deacons and preachers spent the day in a planning session.

— 1997 —

Elders
Stan Bronson
Johnny Davis
Joe Holland
Jerry Hopkins

Evangelists
Dan Jenkins
Dean Reynolds
Ron Brackett
David Sproule, II

Deacons
Bill Boyd
David Brown
Pete Brown
Ron Cullom
Ephriam Davis
Don Dodd
Mike Erickson
Dan Fuller
Jim Howell
Bill Ingram, Sr.
Bill Ingram, Jr.
Gary Jenkins
Jeff Leslie
Dan McLeod
Carl Mack
Joseph Maloney
Greg Morris
Harold Pack
Jerry Pittman
Phil Porter
David Sproule
Scott Studer
Dirk Summerlot
Russell Waggoner

— 1997 —

Baptized (28)

Jan. 12 Brent Leslie
Jan. 15 Harry Galloway
Jan. 26 Scott Brenner
Feb. 09 Michael Burrows
Mar. 04 Silas Moses
Mar. 04 Danielle Carswell
Mar. 06 Hazel McNealy
Mar. 16 Tim Fry
Mar. 20 Betty Redding
Mar. 30 Catherine Seay
Mar. 30 Jesse Avalos
Apr. 06 Renee Artherton
Apr. 13 Diana McArthur
Apr. 27 Pandora Thaxton
July 06 Kelly McClain
Aug. 10 Maxine McCoy
Aug. 16 Sarah Collier
Oct. 05 Verdell Atkins
Oct. 08 Chad Bates
Oct. 09 Andrew Layton
Oct. 19 Timothy Thomas
Oct. 26 Sandra Daniels
Nov. 23 Pam Caudill
Dec. 02 Lucille Wright
Dec. 14 Matthew Phipps
Dec. 21 Hamilton St. Hill
Dec. 21 Jillian Sukanec
Dec. 28 Patricia Ventress

Restored (2)

Feb. 02 Philip Lee Girten, Jr.
Dec. 10 Ken Hirsh, Sr.

Identified (26)

Feb. 02 Mike & Kathy Moore
Feb. 09 Barbara Clark
Feb. 09 Ivor Williams
Mar. 02 Sallie Moses
Mar. 30 Hershel & Mary Katherine Knight
June 29 Scott Hair
July 06 Thelma Hart
July 06 Ilene Edwards
July 16 Shirley Haymin
Aug. 03 Stephen Beliech
Aug. 31 Bud & Annette Schmidt
Oct. 05 Pete & Kristi Harker
Oct. 05 Paul & Maria Jones, Dexter & Darlene
Oct. 12 Glena & Scott Maggart
Nov. 12 Kim Heath
Nov. 16 Duane & Janice Whittington

Weddings (4)

July 11 J.R. McAtee & Corinne Holaday
Aug. 02 Scotty Studer & Allison Ledbetter
Oct. 07 Jeff Heath & Kim McKnight
Dec.   Hamilton St. Hill & Hazel McNealy

Births (3)

Mar. 10 Samuel Grant Moore
Oct. 05 Alexandria Williamson
Nov. 17 Brian Duane Whittington

Total Additions: 56   **245 Families; 410 Members**

— 1997 —

Died (9)
Jan. 14 Bill Reichel
Jan. 21 Earl Girten
Feb. 23 Myrtle Morris
Mar. 28 Norma Marchand
Apr. 26 Ruthie Burgess
May 18 Bill Powell
July 03 Bill Bain
July 27 Lillian Witt
Aug.   Argie Moore

Moved Away (21)
Feb. 09 Janette Grenier
Mar. 09 Mylon & Paula Fulford
Mar. 14 Debbie Kutcher
May 01 Jennifer Jackson
May 07 Scott Brenner
May 11 Susan Freire
May 30 Henry Thomson
June 01 Joyce Parker
July 13 Steven Reeves
July 13 Ivor Williams
July 13 Corinne Holaday
July 13 Scotty Studer
July 13 Merlene Stoker
Aug. 01 John Coppens
Aug. 10 Joyce Bain
Aug. 17 Diana McArthur
Sep. 07 Tumeka Cox
Oct. 31 Jan Conger
Nov. 30 Pete & Kristi Harker

Moved Membership (21)
Jan. 12 Shirley Haymin (Dodd Road)
Jan. 19 Brent & Yvonne Clark (Suncoast)
Feb. 09 Bobbi Ferland (Jupiter)
Feb. 25 Marty Williams (Suncoast)
Mar. 30 Bud & Annette Schmidt (Suncoast)
Apr. 06 Ron & Laverna Cullom (Westside)
Apr. 16 Trina Wright (Westside)
Apr. 20 Teri Jenkins (Westside)
Apr. 27 Barbara & David Jaress (Jupiter)
June 25 David & Carolyn Perkins (Jog Road)
July 13 Doug Lambert (Jupiter)
Aug. 10 Cheryl Daniels & Janelle Ware (S Ave)
Oct. 05 Bentley Utt (Jupiter)
Nov. 16 David & Cathy Payne (Westside)

Total Losses: 73   **245 Families; 410 Members**

— 1998 —

As a congregation, we toured the new building site on January 25.

Paul Jones began a new deaf language class on February 1.

Hardeman Nichols conducted our spring meeting on March 1-5.

Beginning the second week in March, we listened to tapes of the New Testament together as a congregation.

Our Sixteenth Annual Ladies' Day was conducted on March 16 with Barbara Mackifield as the speaker. The theme was "A New Beginning."

A Men's Retreat was held all day on April 25 at the building. The theme was "Tear Off the Roof."

The annual Junior/Senior Banquet was held on Friday, May 1 at the Double Tree Hotel in Fort Lauderdale. The theme was "I Believe." Amanda Shelt was selected as second runner-up to the Queen. Ashlee Hirsh and Sean Saunders received honorable mention.

The annual Widows' Brunch was held on Saturday, May 16 at the home of Judie Jenkins.

We had a Personal Evangelism Workshop conducted by Ed McGeachy of Arlington, Texas on June 26-27. Themes were "Building Bridges" and "Go Make Disciples."

Bill Ingram, Jr. resigned as deacon on July 12 for personal reasons, and Jim Howell moved away on June 21.

Our week at the Central Florida Bible Camp was on July 19-25 with Ron Brackett as director.

Several of our young people taught at the Stuart Vacation Bible School on July 29-August 2.

We had a youth rally on August 7-8 with David Baker from Savannah, Tennessee.

September 19 was "G.S.U.D." at the new building. Many of our members helped to lay sod on "Green Side Up Day."

Randall Hunter began selecting those to serve at the Lord's table and lead prayer on September 19.

The final service at the old building and the first service in the new building was on October 11.

Many of our members participated in door-knocking around the new building on October 17 and October 24.

On November 15, the elders, deacons and preachers spent the day in a planning session.

— 1998 —

The Third Annual South Florida Lectureship, entitled "Fundamentals of Our Faith" was conducted on November 6-8. Keynote speakers were Dan Jenkins (Palm Beach Lakes); Boyd Williams (Vero Beach); David Shanks (Overton, Miami); David Sproule, II (Palm Beach Lakes); and Lawrence Gilmore (Westside). Song leaders were Larry Porter (Jupiter/Tequesta); Wes Holland (Palm Beach Lakes); David Brooker (Vero Beach); and Jerry Hopkins (Palm Beach Lakes). Teaching classes were Ronnie Crocker (Jupiter/Tequesta); Stan Bronson (Palm Beach Lakes); Don Jones (Okeechobee); James Boyd (McMinnville, Tennessee); Henry McFadden (Lake Street, Stuart); Bill Boyd (Palm Beach Lakes); Ernest Mackifield (Third Street); Gary Davenport (West Broward); Frank Parker (Fairmont Drive); Jerry Hopkins (Palm Beach Lakes); Ron Brackett (Palm Beach Lakes); Bill Nicks (Jupiter/Tequesta); Gary Jenkins (Palm Beach Lakes); I.C. Spivey (Lake Ida); Benny Santiago (Dodd Road); Jeanie Langford (Jupiter/Tequesta); and Terry Frizzell (Jupiter/Tequesta). In addition, there was a panel of elders from Palm Beach Lakes, Suncoast and Jupiter/Tequesta for a Questions & Answers session. The lectureship was very well supported by other congregations in the area.

Dean Reynolds passed away on December 22. Dean had been working with the congregation for 24 years since August 1, 1974.

Elders	**Deacons**	**Deacons (cont.)**
Stan Bronson	Bill Boyd	Dan McLeod
Johnny Davis	David Brown	Carl Mack
Joe Holland	Pete Brown	Joseph Maloney
Jerry Hopkins	Ron Cullom	Greg Morris
	Ephriam Davis	Harold Pack
Evangelists	Don Dodd	Jerry Pittman
Dan Jenkins	Mike Erickson	Phil Porter
Ron Brackett	Dan Fuller	David Sproule
David Sproule, II	Bill Ingram, Sr.	Scott Studer
	Gary Jenkins	Dirk Summerlot
	Jeff Leslie	Russell Waggoner

— 1998 —

Baptized (14)
Jan. 04 Janine Machan
Jan. 25 Janice Reynolds
Feb. 15 Peggy Jackson
May 24   Amy Ehrmantraut
June 21 Beth Pittman
June 29 Roges Exhaus
June 29 Camele Sinclair
July 19 Jimmy Banks
Sep. 11 Mike Fanale
Nov. 13 Leslie Williams
Nov. 15 Katie Feeney
Nov. 22 Chuck Forest
Nov. 26 Lisa Holaday
Dec. 03 Quinntel Smith

Restored (2)
Sep. 11 Patty Fanale
Oct. 04 Kelvin Samuel

Weddings (2)
Mar. 21 Randall Hunter & Renee Artherton
July 07 Chris Erickson & Amy Ehrmantraut

Births (1)
Oct. 23 Antionette Jasmine Charles

Identified (35)
Mar. 01 J.B. Tucker
Mar. 08 Mark Dunaway
Apr. 12 Tumeka Cox
May 24   Harold & Margaret Wade
May 31   Terry Gardner
July 05 Sherry Gibson
July 19 Leonard Williams
July 19 Joseph & Anthioda Charles
July 19 Joseph & Marie Charles
Aug. 03 Karen (Ally) Alberga
Aug. 09 Pat Tallman
Aug. 09 Jim Stark
Aug. 09 Jessica Thornton
Aug. 23 Rick & Sherrie Tibbetts
Aug. 30 Chuck Milton
Sep. 13 Byron & Jackie Smith
Sep. 20 Joe, Bettye & Chris Evans
Oct. 11 Jane Camey
Oct. 18 Mike Brown
Oct. 25 Moses & Brenda Johnson
Nov. 15 Bobbi Ferland
Nov. 15 Marty Williams
Dec. 02 Chris & Amy Erickson
Dec. 06 Jimmy & Helen Burney
Dec. 13 Martie Steinmann

Total Additions: 51

— 1998 —

Died (5)
Mar. 30 Dee Manwaring
Aug. 18 Hattie Hopkins
Oct. 05 Bill Tennant
Nov. 30 Tera Green
Dec. 22 Dean Reynolds

Moved Membership (5)
July 12 Timothy Thomas (Westside)
July 13 Peggy & Valerie MacDougal
         (Dodd Road)
Nov. 08 Kevin Wagner (Suncoast)
Dec. 07 Pearl El (Third Street)

Moved Away (27)
Mar. 30 Dot Lang
Apr. 24 Mike & Kathy Moore
Apr. 24 Scott Hair
May 03   John & Annette Gaessler
May 10   J.B. Tucker
May 24   Andrea & Troy Spradlin
May 24   Hamilton & Hazel St. Hill
May 24   Clara Bond
June 07 Danielle Carswell
June 14 Chris Erickson
June 14 Amy Ehrmantraut
June 21 Jim & Judy Howell
July 26 Mark Dunaway
Aug. 30 Don & Pam Williams
Oct. 25 Mike & Patty Fanale
Oct. 25 Joyce Marshall
Oct. 28 Ken, Lynne, & Ashlee Hirsh
Oct. 31 Jessica Thornton

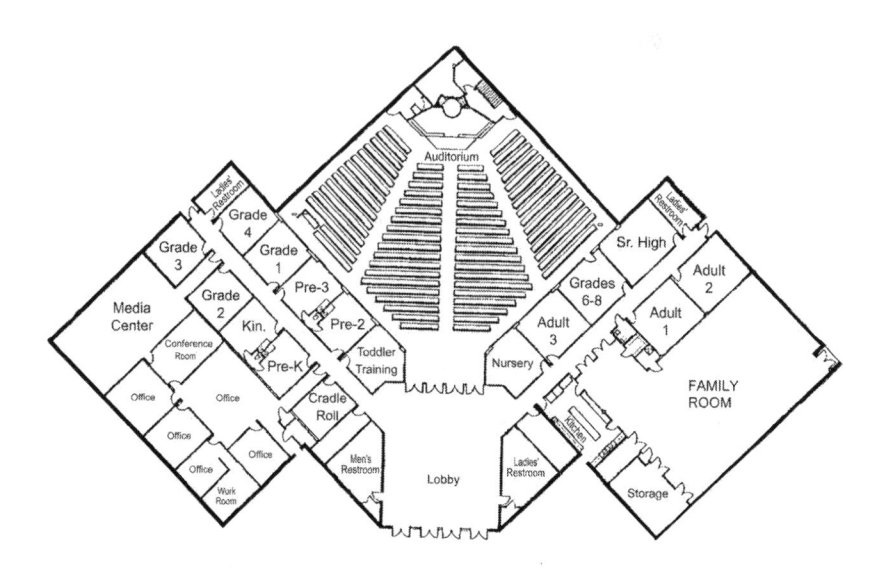

Total Losses: 52   **248 Families; 411 Members**

— 1999 —

Ralph Gilmore from Jackson, Tennessee was our speaker for an "End Times Seminar" conducted on January 15-17.

Our spring Gospel Meeting was conducted by Dave Miller from Bedford, Texas on February 28-March 4.

Our Twenty-Third Annual Sweetheart Banquet hosted by the Senior High youth for the Pioneers was held on Sunday, February 14 following morning worship. The theme was "Superheroes and Villains."

The annual Newcomers' Banquet was hosted by Area 2 on Friday, March 12.

Sixteen of our members, directed by David Sproule, II, went on a Trinidad Mission Trip to the San Fernando church of Christ on March 13-20.

Our Seventeenth Annual Ladies' Day was held on Thursday, April 15, with Jean Reel, from Lake Placid, as the speaker.

Our Third Annual Men's Retreat was on Saturday, May 8. The theme was "Full Steam Ahead."

The annual Junior/Senior Banquet was held at the Ibis Golf and Country Club on Friday, May 14. Ryan Brackett was chosen King.

Jerry Jenkins from Birmingham, Alabama was our speaker for the Family Seminar on Friday-Sunday, May 21-23

Our teens conducted a Vacation Bible School in Roxboro, North Carolina during the week of July 18.

July 18-24 was our week at the Central Florida Bible Camp conducted by Ron Brackett.

Dominic Dos Santos from Trinidad was our speaker for a Youth Summit on August 27-29. The theme was "Dare to Be Different."

Dr. Bert Thompson from Montgomery, Alabama conducted our Creation/Evolution Seminar on Friday through Sunday, August 27-29.

Joe Maloney resigned as a deacon for health reasons on October 3.

The Junior High youth hosted a Luau for the Pioneers on Saturday, October 23.

Our Fourth Annual South Florida Lectureship entitled "Life & Godliness" was held on November 12-14. Keynote speakers were Dan Jenkins (Palm Beach Lakes); Jonathan Jenkins (Decatur, Georgia); David Shanks (Overton, Miami); Boyd Williams (Vero Beach); and Robert Martin (Pacific Islands). Song leaders were Larry Porter (Jupiter/Tequesta); George Barber (West Broward); David Brooker (Vero Beach); Dan Jenkins (Palm Beach Lakes);

— 1999 —

and Benny Santiago (Dodd Road). Teaching classes were Bill Boyd (Palm Beach Lakes); Billy Davidson (Clearwater); Allan Jenkins (Midway Road, Ft. Pierce); James Haymin (Palm Beach Lakes); David Sproule, II (Palm Beach Lakes); Don Jones (Okeechobee); Clifford Reel (Lake Placid); Leon Green (Lake Street, Stuart); Vic Pruett (Vero Beach); Ernest & Barbara Mackifield (Third Street); Stan Bronson (Palm Beach Lakes); Jimmy McDowell (Jupiter/Tequesta); Frank Parker (Sebring); John Hoelzer (Palm Beach Lakes); Ron Brackett (Palm Beach Lakes); Terry Frizzell (Jupiter/Tequesta); Lawrence Gilmore (Westside); Benny Santiago (Dodd Road); and Ronnie Crocker (Stuart).

Elders
Stan Bronson
Johnny Davis
Joe Holland
Jerry Hopkins

Evangelists
Dan Jenkins
Ron Brackett
David Sproule, II

Deacons
Bill Boyd
David Brown
Pete Brown
Ron Cullom
Ephriam Davis
Don Dodd
Mike Erickson
Dan Fuller
Bill Ingram, Sr.
Gary Jenkins
Jeff Leslie
Dan McLeod
Carl Mack
Greg Morris
Harold Pack
Jerry Pittman
Phil Porter
David Sproule
Scott Studer
Dirk Summerlot
Russell Waggoner

— 1999 —

Baptized (26)
Jan. 10 Shelly Hines
Jan. 17 Brittany Milton
Jan. 24 Jamey Steinmann
Jan. 24 Lindsey Jenkins
Jan. 24 Kelsey Ingram
Jan. 25 Joe Gibson
Mar. 05 John Slattery
Mar. 07 Jonathan Erickson
Mar. 17 Michael Spall
Apr. 11 Kevin Schlueter
Apr. 25 Quinntavias Smith
May 02 Cornelius Brown
May 05 Heather Longhenry
May 16 Mike Damron
June 28 Hazel Collier
July 07 Sonia Ocasio
July 11 Julio Vasquez
July 22 Hazel Hackshaw
July 25 LaKeysha Williams-Brown
Aug. 15 Brittney Steinmann
Aug. 19 Marie Shoff
Aug. 29 Kyle Milton
Sep. 05 Don Barrow
Sep. 05 Gabrielle Reeves
Oct. 01 Juanita Cozart
Oct. 21 Gary Humphries

Weddings (1)
May 01 Chad Bates & Christina Colage

Births (2)
May 28 Lauren Erickson
Oct. 24 Lydia Quinn

— 1999 —

Identified (45)

Jan. 31 Don & Ruth Ann Rankey
Jan. 31 Joey Tipton
Jan. 31 Aaron Cozart
Feb. 07 Becky Hopper
Feb. 07 Tom & Bonalee Kreinberg
Feb. 21 Ed & Helen Bashaw
Feb. 21 Vann & Vicky Black
Feb. 21 Al & Rhonda Washington
Feb. 28 Doris Seay
Mar. 05 Jennie Slattery
Mar. 07 Sara Crocker
Mar. 07 David Milton
Mar. 14 Peter Williams
Mar. 21 Roy Crocker
Apr. 11 Leesa Shenk
Apr. 11 Goodness Akandu
Apr. 18 Trina Wright
May 23 Doug Carrick
May 23 Janetta Green
May 23 Joe Terry
May 30 Roy Sovine
June 06 Gary Lewandowski
June 13 Suzanne Halsell
July 04 Mary Rudy
Aug. 08 John, Regina, Heather & Melissa Mayne
Aug. 22 Nicole Freseman
Aug. 26 Cleave Pamphile
Sep. 12 Maureen Machan, Danny & Keri
Nov. 14 Mary Jackson
Nov. 28 Charley & Petra Carter

Identified (cont.)

Dec. 08 Leo Garcia
Dec. 12 Marilyn Dixon
Dec. 12 Lynne Lawson
Dec. 26 Tasha Bridgett

Total Additions: 71   **242 Families; 420 Members**

— 1999 —

Died (7)
Feb. 14 Harold Wade
Feb. 19 Bette McMasters
June 07 Hazel Manwaring
Aug. 20 Irene Morlock
Oct. 22 Lee Sherrod
Dec. 12 Clarence Dixon
Dec. 16 Ann Bone

Moved Away (36)
Jan. 03 Duane & Janice Whittington
Jan. 03 Ken Hirsh, Jr.
Jan. 24 Irene Williams
Feb. 19 Irene Dallas
Apr. 19 Jessie Lawson
June 01 Richard Sineath
June 01 Michael Spall
June 08 Art, Gina, Diana, Kathy & Kelly Tek
June 08 Mandy Strickland
June 08 Shannon Stroh
June 20 Bud & Annette Schmidt
July 04 Joe, Bettye, & Chris Evans
July 11 Goodness Akandu
July 11 Tasha Bridgett
Aug. 15 Kevin Schlueter
Aug. 22 Randall & Renee Hunter
Sep. 05 Vann & Vicky Black
Oct. 24 Eileen Rogers
Nov. 30 Paul, Maria, Dexter & Darlene Jones
Dec. 07 Bobbi Ferland
Dec. 21 Joey Tipton
Dec. 26 Jim & Margie Cunningham

Moved Membership (7)
Jan. 25 Byron & Jackie Smith (Suncoast)
Aug. 01 Ally Alberga (Suncoast)
Aug. 29 Opal Powell (Dodd Road)
Oct. 24 Don Barrow (Jupiter/Tequesta)
Nov. 21 Gary Lewandowski (Suncoast)
Dec. 26 Joe Terry (Jupiter/Tequesta)

Total Losses: 64   **242 Families; 420 Members**

— 2000 —

Three of our deacons moved away: David Sproule on January 3; Ephraim Davis on February 27; and Bill Boyd on June 1.

The elders, deacons and preachers had a planning session on January 14-15 at a camp on the west coast. The elders turned more responsibility over to the deacons.

Our annual Newcomers' Banquet was on January 28.

The Twenty-Fourth Annual Sweetheart Banquet for the Pioneers was hosted by the Senior High youth on February 13.

Our spring Gospel Meeting was on March 5-9 with Tom Holland from Brentwood, Tennessee as the speaker.

The Eighteenth Annual Ladies' Day was on April 13 with Jeanie Langford as the speaker. The theme was "Lord, Teach Me To Pray."

The Junior/Senior Banquet was on April 28. Allison Price was first runner-up to the Queen; Shelly Roberts won the Best Theme Award; and Brad Shelt was second runner-up to the King.

A marriage seminar entitled "Putting the Music Back in Your Marriage" was held on May 12- 14 with Glenn Colley as the speaker.

The Senior High hosted the Widows' Brunch on May 20 in the Family Room.

Our Senior High youth taught in three Vacation Bible Schools this summer: Lake Placid, Belle Glade and Roxboro, North Carolina.

A one-day Vacation Bible School was held on Saturday, August 5.

The annual Youth Summit entitled "Escape" was held on August 11-12 with Kyle Butt from Montgomery, Alabama as the speaker.

Dan McLeod was ordained as an elder on Sunday, August 13.

Friendship Weekend was held on August 26-27 with Don & Jane McWhorter.

Four more men were appointed as deacons on Sunday, September 24: Novel Brown, Rick Hall, John Mayne and Buzz Nelson.

Spiritual Enrichment Weekend (SEW) was held on October 20-22 at the Lion's Camp in Lakeland.

The elders designated a day of planning during the Bible study hour on October 29. Members gave suggestions about the work to be done by this congregation during the next year.

Bill Ingram, Sr. resigned as deacon on November 12 after serving this congregation for many years as both deacon and elder.

— 2000 —

Our Fifth Annual South Florida Lectureship entitled "Worship That Pleases God" was held on November 10-12. Keynote speakers were Wendell Winkler (Tuscaloosa, Alabama); Dan Jenkins (Palm Beach Lakes); Tom Holland (Brentwood, Tennessee); and Everett Chambers (Bedford, Texas). Dwight Lanham (Franklin, Tennessee) was the song leader for the entire Lectureship. Teaching classes were Ernest Mackifield (West Palm Beach); Earl Edwards (Henderson, Tennessee); Lawrence Gilmore (Westside); Gary Davenport (West Broward); Terry Frizzell (Jupiter/Tequesta); Bob Bauer (Belle Glade); and Steve Ellis (Jupiter/Tequesta).

Elders
Stan Bronson
Johnny Davis
Joe Holland
Jerry Hopkins
Dan McLeod

Evangelists
Dan Jenkins
Ron Brackett
David Sproule, II

Deacons
David Brown
Novel Brown
Pete Brown
Ron Cullom
Don Dodd
Mike Erickson
Dan Fuller
Rick Hall
Gary Jenkins
Jeff Leslie
Carl Mack
John Mayne
Greg Morris
Buzz Nelson
Harold Pack
Jerry Pittman
Phil Porter
Scott Studer
Dirk Summerlot
Russell Waggoner

— 2000 —

Baptized (35)
Feb. 03 Shawn Mitchell
Feb. 13 Cathy Zubriski
Feb. 27 Darin Summerlot
Mar. 03 Zac Humphries
Mar. 07 Valerie Humphries
Mar. 12 Betty Nathanson
Mar. 22 Pete Zubriski
Apr. 14 Brian Drumheller
June 14 Samantha Eutsey
June 14 Altagrace Marie Charles
June 18 Rebecca Lorenzana
June 25 Jackie Creary
July 19 Heather Morris
July 28 Jack Charles (camp)
July 28 Hector Rene Rivera (camp)
July 28 Samantha Stowe (camp)
July 30 Katie Weizer
Aug. 06 Michael Gamble
Aug. 06 Cecil Felkner
Aug. 09 Taylor Reeves
Aug. 20 Christopher Jacquot
Aug. 20 Lisa Eutsey
Sep. 10 Alejandra Cifuentes (Ale)
Sep. 17 Jim McFadden
Sep. 17 Frederick Key
Sep. 17 Jelynne Carswell
Sep. 20 Nicole Chapman
Sep. 24 Bryan Zerfas
Oct. 15 Tommy Byrd
Oct. 15 Sharon Jean Louis
Oct. 22 Rubin Hugee
Oct. 29 Bobby Townsend
Dec. 03 Kahla King

Baptized (cont.)
Dec. 31 Jennifer Carver
Dec. 31 Carsenna Cummings

Restored (4)
Feb. 06 Beau Nelson
Mar. 12 Philip Girten, Jr.
Apr. 02 Jeremiah Cummings
Sep. 03 Caraline Wedges

Weddings (3)
Mar. 25 Chris Fry & Vickie Lane
June 10 Bill Ingram, Jr. & Gai Reeves
July 14 Rudolph March & Verdell Atkins

Births (5)
Feb. 14 Richard Charles
June 01 Austin James Williams
June 20 Lillian Banks
June 22 Anna Kathryn Gibson
Sep. 08 Katie Nicole Sproule

— 2000 —

Identified (52)

Jan. 02	David & Renee Peace
Jan. 12	Juli Cartwright
Feb. 06	Pearl El
Feb. 20	Damian & Sophia Fletcher
Feb. 27	John & Carolyn Kemp
Mar. 26	Amy Newman
Apr. 09	Dick & Marcia Kelley
Apr. 12	Bertha Sharpe
Apr. 16	Joyce Parker
Apr. 30	Bertie O'Grady
July 05	Bob & Sandy DeVall
July 09	Darrell & Nancy Blaylock
July 16	Jacade & Susan Reynolds
July 16	Jim, Kim & Lindsey Leslie
July 16	Hector & Ele Rivera
July 16	Cindy Helwig
July 30	Carolyn Moore
Aug. 06	Linda Felkner
Aug. 13	Jeannie Buonadonna
Aug. 13	Vera Oliver
Aug. 16	Lennie Langley
Aug. 30	Kevin & Angie Vanderwende
Sep. 10	Lee & Tori Boyd
Sep. 17	Sebrina Key
Sep. 17	Ray Seay
Sep. 17	Billie Jo Sanderson
Oct. 15	Juanita Huser
Oct. 22	Maggie Sawick
Oct. 25	Beverly Bostic
Oct. 29	Lloyd & Jalene Moody
Nov. 12	Randall & Renee Hunter
Dec. 03	Jennifer Anderson
Dec. 03	Kenva Delancey

Identified (cont.)

Dec. 17	David, Cathy & Andrew Payne
Dec. 31	James A. Cochran
Dec. 31	William D. Shake

Total Additions: 91   **268 Families; 458 Members**

— 2000 —

Died (2)
Jan. 03 Ann Haines
Jan. 08 Ben Gardner

Moved Away (30)
Jan. 03 David & Bette Sproule
Feb. 27 Ephriam & Donna Davis
Mar. 12 Cleave Pamphile
Mar. 19 Tom & Bonalee Kreinberg
Mar. 25 Chris Fry
Mar. 26 Amy Affron
Apr. 11 Leo Garcia
Apr. 11 Thelma Hart
Apr. 29 Jane Carney
June 01 Bill, Lori, Rose & Cliff Boyd
June 12 Wes Holland
June 26 David & Renee Peace
July 18 Joe & Sherry Gibson
Aug. 30 Aaron & Juanita Cozart
Oct. 29 Bryan Zerfas
Nov. 19 Aren Elizee
Dec. 11 Becky Hopper
Dec. 11 Jacade & Susan Reynolds
Dec. 24 Gary Humphries
Dec. 31 Megan Cox

Moved Membership (6)
May 10 Norman & Marie Smedley (Jupiter)
Aug. 27 John & Jennie Slattery (Jupiter)
Nov. 01 Barbara Clark (Okeechobee)
Dec. 17 Brad Shelt (Stuart)

Total Losses: 43   268 Families; 458 Members

— 2001 —

The Twenty-Fifth Annual Sweetheart Banquet for the Pioneers was hosted by the Senior High youth on February 11.

Our spring Gospel Meeting was on March 11-15 with Ralph Gilmore from Henderson, Tennessee as the speaker on Sunday-Wednesday, and William Miller from Nassau, Bahamas was the speaker on Thursday.

Carl Mack resigned as deacon on April 15 because of health reasons.

A new pictorial church membership was issued on April 15.

The Nineteenth Annual Ladies' Day was on April 19 with Julie Jenkins as the speaker. The theme was "Because He Lives."

A "Reaching the Lost and Wayward" Seminar was held on May 11-13 with Bob Danklefsen as the speaker.

The Junior/Senior Banquet was on May 11. Trey Ingram was first runner-up to the King and Juli Cartwright, Heather Mayne, Heather Morris and Amber Pittman received honorable mention.

Ryan Brackett worked for the church during summer vacation from Freed-Hardeman University.

David Sproule took ten of our teens on a mission trip to Anderson, South Carolina on June 15-22 where they did door-knocking and taught VBS.

A Future Preacher's Training Camp was held at the building on June 27-July 1.

David Sproule took eleven of our teens on a mission trip to Freeport, Bahamas on July 14-21.

The Agape Groups were changed on July 1 from fifteen groups to nine.

Our week at Central Florida Bible Camp with Ron Brackett as director was held on July 22-28.

The Sixth Annual Youth Summit entitled "CPR for Choking Christians" was held on August 10-12 with Dale Jenkins from Nashville, Tennessee as the speaker.

There was a Bible School Teacher Workshop on September 15-16 with Paul Brown and Debbie Bumbalough.

A Young Ladies' Camp was conducted at the building on September 28-29.

Robert & Mary Martin were here on October 14 to give a report on their work in the Pacific Islands.

Spiritual Enrichment Weekend was conducted on October 19-21 at

— 2001 —

the 4-H Camp in Sebring.

Input Sunday was on October 28 during the regular Bible study hour to allow members to give input to the elders for things to be done next year.

The Sixth Annual South Florida Lectureship entitled "Here Am I, Send Me" was conducted on November 9-11. Out of town speakers were Bill Craddock, Ronnie Crocker, Roy Lanier, Jr., Robert & Mary Martin, Bill Nicks, Eric Owens, Frank Parker and Dominic Dos Santos.

The elders, deacons and preachers had a planning retreat at the building on Friday-Saturday, November 30-December 1.

Elders
Stan Bronson
Johnny Davis
Joe Holland
Jerry Hopkins
Dan McLeod

Evangelists
Dan Jenkins
Ron Brackett
David Sproule, II

Deacons
David Brown
Novel Brown
Pete Brown
Ron Cullom
Don Dodd
Mike Erickson
Dan Fuller
Rick Hall
Gary Jenkins
Jeff Leslie
John Mayne
Greg Morris
Buzz Nelson
Harold Pack
Jerry Pittman
Phil Porter
Scott Studer
Dirk Summerlot
Russell Waggoner

— 2001 —

Baptized (30)

Jan. 02	Anna Marie Blaylock
Jan. 21	Hugh Sharpe
Jan. 20	Sallye Carswell
Jan. 29	Terry Denton
Jan. 30	Richard R. Haines, Sr.
Feb. 11	Patricia Humphries
Feb. 18	Emily Cox
Feb. 25	Nathaniel Nelson
Mar. 02	Audrey Callebot
Mar. 18	Gene Ainsworth
Mar. 25	Michell Castonguay
Mar. 28	Ken Veverka
Apr. 01	Shoshanna Mickens
June 03	Michelle Hackshaw
June 10	Nikki Hahn
July 01	Sarah E. Smith
July 08	Pam Smith
July 15	Lynniese Worthington
July 27	Daniel Payne
July 27	LaToya Ratliff
July 29	Julie Charles
Aug. 01	Stacy Hall
Aug. 29	Casey Byerly
Sep. 28	Carrie LaConte
Oct. 08	Jean C. Duperat
Oct. 21	Diane Seegers
Nov. 04	Rosemarie Joseph
Dec. 02	Terrie Flynn
Dec. 09	Bernadette Duperat
Dec. 24	Meredith Blaylock

Identified (52)

Jan. 31	Alvin & Judy Leaks
Feb. 11	Alvin, April, & Kyle Smith
Feb. 25	Saul Ellis
Mar. 25	Floyd & Curtis Booth
Apr. 15	Patricia Eccles
Apr. 18	David & Charlene May
Apr. 18	Freddy & Tori Shelley
Apr. 29	Joe & Cathy Peterson
Apr. 29	Elizabeth Trejo
May 27	Lynn Brown
June 03	Reba Little
June 17	Harold & Donna Armstrong
June 17	Tina Lang
June 20	Seth Watson
July 01	Bryan & Beth Bonner
July 15	Richard, Debi & Matthew Watson
July 15	Jim & Connye Plouffe
July 22	Steve & Nohemi Rios
July 29	Racquel Humphrey
Sep. 02	Rick & Linda Alexander
Sep. 09	Sandi & Daniel Lomeli
Sep. 16	Jerri, Cheri & Jodi Flatt
Oct. 05	Ron, Josh & Robert Lupo
Oct. 14	Jennifer Brown
Oct. 28	Pedro & Cathrilla Barajas
Nov. 18	Paul, Kim, Mindy & Jackie Hensel
Nov. 18	Gary Lewandowski
Dec. 23	Darin Height
Dec. 30	Enrique Chow Ingle

— 2001 —

Restored (4)
Aug. 05 Caraline Wedges
Sep. 30 Jim Shiver
Oct. 28 Jeff & Kim Heath

Weddings (7)
Mar. 03 Craig Campbell & Nicole Colage
June 02 Brad Costello & Amanda Shelt
July 07 Saul Ellis & Becky Brackett
Aug. 04 Sharah Larson & Justin Collier
Sep. 25 Ken Veverka & Martie Steinmann
Nov. 03 Kelly McClain & Michelle Marcello
Nov. 05 Stan Cochran & Bari Bliss

Births (4)
Apr. 29 Mariah Mickens
May 16 Alvin Leaks, Jr.
Oct. 25 Jalen Lamar Johnson
Nov. 24 Kelly Danielle Sproule

Total Additions: 86   **287 Families; 483 Members**

— 2001 —

Died (4)
Mar. 07 Hardy Cooper
Mar. 11 Roy Crocker
Apr. 11 Hugh Sharpe
July 30 Shirley Haymin

Moved Away (29)
Mar. 08 Kevin & Angie Vanderwende
Mar. 25 Kathy Dean (GA)
Mar. 25 Katie Weizer (Okeechobee)
Apr. 08 Virginia Warner (Suncoast)
June 02 Amanda Shelt
June 24 Rebecca Lorenzana & Bobby (Ft. Pierce)
July 03 Bertie O'Grady (VT)
July 10 Reba Little (Alabama)
July 10 Zachary Humphries (AL)
July 15 Matthew King (Tampa)
Aug. 04 Justin Collier
Aug. 12 Tim Mahlbacher (Orlando)
Aug. 12 Chris & Amy Erickson (TN)
Sep. 23 Dianna Girten (Bronson, FL)
Sep. 26 Lee, Tori & Tommy Byrd (Tampa)
Oct. 08 Wayne & Margie Fortenberry (Okeechobee)
Oct. 14 James Cochran (IN)
Oct. 14 Alvin & Judy Leaks (Ft. Laud.)
Oct. 14 Sarah Smith
Nov. 16 John & Louise Weisenburger (GA)
Dec. 09 Phil Girten (Bronson, FL)

Total Losses: 52   **287 Families; 483 Members**

— 2002 —

A Brecheen/Faulkner Marriage Enrichment Seminar was held on January 18-20. They also spoke Sunday at both morning services.

A party was held on Sunday, February 17 for Dan & Judie Jenkins, celebrating twenty years of service at Palm Beach Lakes.

Our spring Gospel Meeting was on March 3-7 with Richard Melson of Dayton, Ohio as the speaker.

Twenty of our members went on a campaign to Trinidad on March 23-30.

Our Twentieth Annual Ladies' Day was held on April 18 with Laurel Sewell as the speaker. The theme was "Gifts of Hospitality."

The annual Junior/Senior Banquet was held at the Embassy Suites in Palm Beach Gardens on April 19. David Milton was awarded the title of King, and Kelly Affron was awarded the title of Queen and also won the award for best theme.

Alan Highers conducted an "Issues Facing the Church" seminar on May 17-19.

Trey Ingram worked for the church during the summer vacation from Freed-Hardeman University.

Ten young men attended the Future Preachers' Training Camp held on June 12-15. They conducted all the services on Sunday, June 16.

David Sproule took ten of our teens on a mission trip to Virginia Beach, Virginia on June 21-28 to conduct a VBS and hand out flyers.

David Sproule took thirteen of our young people to Lake Placid on July 13-18 to conduct a VBS.

Our week at Central Florida Bible Camp, with Ron Brackett as director, was held on July 21-27.

Al & Rhonda Washington moved to Austin, Texas in August to begin training to become a preacher.

A Leadership Training Camp for Young Women was conducted at our building on August 2-3.

The Seventh Annual Youth Summit, entitled "Evangelizing Your World," conducted by Chris Fry was held on August 9-10. At the same time, a Leadership Forum entitled, "The Nuts and Bolts of Leadership," was conducted by J.J. Turner.

Two deacons resigned on September 15: Russell Waggoner because of poor health, and John Mayne because of personal reasons. His job is taking

— 2002 —

him out of town a lot.

The Family Bible Bowl was held on October 5.

Spiritual Enrichment Weekend was conducted on October 18-20 at the Lions' Camp in Lake Wales.

A new pictorial directory was issued on November 3.

The Seventh Annual South Florida Lectureship, entitled "Applying Acts in the Twenty-First Century," was held on November 8-10. Keynote speakers were Dan Jenkins, Eric Owens, Hardeman Nichols, and David Sproule, II. Breakout classes were conducted by Benny Santiago, Jr., Steve Ellis, Joe Holland, David Lipe, Bill & Lori Boyd, Gary Davenport, Perry Hall, Allan Jenkins, Ernest Mackifield, Frank Parker, Dan McLeod, Al Washington, Jonathan Jenkins, and Ron Brackett.

Elders
Stan Bronson
Johnny Davis
Joe Holland
Jerry Hopkins
Dan McLeod

Evangelists
Dan Jenkins
Ron Brackett
David Sproule, II

Deacons
David Brown
Novel Brown
Pete Brown
Ron Cullom
Don Dodd
Mike Erickson
Dan Fuller
Rick Hall
Gary Jenkins
Jeff Leslie
Greg Morris
Buzz Nelson
Harold Pack
Jerry Pittman
Phil Porter
Scott Studer
Dirk Summerlot

— 2002 —

Baptized (39)
Jan. 18 Christine Pavek
Jan. 20 Michael Lupo
Jan. 27 Mark Hartwig
Feb. 24 April Dougherty
Feb. 27 Angel Fusco
Mar. 03 Stephanie Hensel
Mar. 05 Shea Brown
Mar. 07 Andrew Sobieraj
Mar. 10 Rachel Fuller
Mar. 10 Bethany Leslie
Mar. 10 Julie Leslie
Mar. 24 Solomon Robinson, Jr.
Mar. 24 John Hoelzer, Jr.
Mar. 31 Rachel Byerly
Mar. 31 Michael Curington
Apr. 03 Valerie Porter
Apr. 17 Jim Winkle
May 01 Alphonso Paul
May 01 Trenise Thomas
June 09 John Seegers
June 26 Stahia Young
June 28 Benjamin Pratt
June 28 Godfrey Pratt
July 28 Jenifer Flatt
July 28 Brittney Humphries
July 29 Willie Wilkins
July 29 LaToya Pringley
Aug. 03 Patricia Hackshaw
Aug. 04 Courtney Evans
Aug. 11 Rose Williams
Aug. 11 Briana Buckhalter
Sep. 18 Daniel Jenkins
Oct. 27 Macey Leslie

Baptized (cont.)
Nov. 03 Kim Worthington
Dec. 24 Kevin Rolston
Dec. 24. Kim Palacios
Dec. 28 Justin Maloney
Dec. 29 Vivian Clements
Dec. 29 Debbie Van Oort

Identified (31)
Jan. 16 Remy Elius
Mar. 17 Steven Reeves
Apr. 07 Lydia Davidson
May 05 Angela, Shawna & Jessica Fasig
May 12 Bob Fasig
May 19 Jeff & Jennifer Goodale
June 09 Brian, Jenni & Meredith Jones
June 16 Stephanie Hamlen
June 16 Kevin Weeks
June 30 Matt Ellis
July 03 Christine Ellis
July 03 Javier Trilla
July 21 Chuck & Trish Clark
Aug. 11 Anthony Irvin
Aug. 18 Brad & Amanda Costello
Sep. 15 John H. Elliott, Jr.
Sep. 22 Sammy & Peggy Jackson
Oct. 16 Dan Richardson
Dec. 08 Ivan, Lenis, Keila, & Ivan Jr. Villard
Dec. 15 Gloria Denson

— 2002 —

Restored (5)
Jan. 16   Alicia Henderson
Jan. 20   Ruth Lipford
Feb. 24   LaDawn Collier
June 16   Michael Gamble
Aug. 18   Willie Cox

Weddings (9)
May   St. Ruis Vertu & Rosemarie Joseph
May 25   Tom Chadwick & Sarah
June 14   Sean Saunders & Kim Cooper
June 22   Erik Peffer & Jennifer Brown
July 05   Anthony Brown & Jodi Flatt
July 13   Barrett Thompson & Liz Erickson
Aug. 16   Anthony Irvin & Racquel Humphrey
Sep. 28   Dan Richardson & Emily Hopkins
Dec. 27   Kevin Rolston & Kim Palacios

Births (5)
June 19   Abi Emily Rios
Aug. 26   Jayden Kristopher McClain
Oct. 12   Kaitlyn Mayne
Dec. 13   Damond Mickens
Dec. 17   Dylan Kai Heath

Total Additions: 75   **283 Families; 491 Members**

— 2002 —

Died (8)
Jan. 04 Amos Shiver
Feb. 10 Vera Oliver
June 11 Edna Williams
Aug. 18 Betty Harrison
Aug. 22 Kyle Smith
Sep. 04 Erma Hill
Nov. 19 Russell Waggoner
Dec. 15 Audrey Archer

Moved Membership (7)
Apr. 16 Bertha Sharpe (Lake Ida)
Apr. 16 Gary Lewandowski (Suncoast)
Apr. 21 Darrell Young (Suncoast)
Aug. 04 Beverly Bostic (Third Street)
Aug. 11 Chip Carmack (Suncoast)
Oct. 20 Randall & Renee Hunter (Stuart)

Moved Away (17)
Jan. 23 Tina Lang
Feb. 24 Mike Brown
Apr. 30 Emily Cox
May 12 Marc Brown
May 21 Marilou Shiver
June 02 Roy Sovine
June 23 LaDawn Collier
June 23 Carrie LaConte
June 23 Enrique Chow
July 13 Elizabeth Erickson
July 17 Damian & Sophia Fletcher
Aug. 07 Al & Rhonda Washington
Aug. 25 Amy Newman
Sep. 22 Keri Machan
Nov. 04 Tasha Bridgett

Total Losses: 60   **283 Families; 491 Members**

— 2003 —

Friends & Family Day was held on January 26 with a record attendance in this building of 653.

The Twenty-Seventh Annual Sweetheart Banquet hosted by the Senior High youth for the Pioneers was on February 16.

Our spring Gospel Meeting was on March 2-6 with Glenn Colley as the speaker.

The Sonshine Singers from Freed-Hardeman University sang for us after services on Wednesday, March 19.

Four new deacons were appointed on March 30: Tim Fry, Brian Jones, Willie Smith and Richard Watson.

The speaker for the Twenty-First Annual Ladies' Day on April 24 was Rose Coleman. The theme was "God's Woman."

The annual Junior/Senior Banquet was held at the Miami Airport Hilton in Miami on Friday, May 2. Melissa Mayne was awarded the title of Queen and Beth Pittman as first runner-up. Matt Ellis was selected as first runner-up to the King and also won the award for the best theme entitled "Wherever You Will Go." Josh Lupo received honorable mention.

A "Bible and Science Seminar" was conducted by Dr. Bert Thompson on May 9-11.

Johnny Davis resigned as elder on May 18 after serving since 1976 and as deacon since 1964.

David Lipe from Freed-Hardeman University conducted an "Interpreting the Bible Seminar" on May 30-June 1.

Ten of our teens conducted a mission trip to Franklin, NC on June 6-13, and ten more went to North Little Rock, Arkansas on June 23-30.

On July 9-13, the Third Annual Leadership Training Camp for Young Men was conducted.

On August 1-3, the Third Annual Training Camp for Young Women was conducted.

One of our deacons, Brian Jones, moved away on August 7.

A combined Leadership Forum by J.J. Turner and a Youth Forum by Eric Lyons was held on August 8-10.

A Spanish work began in our building in August being taught by Steve Rios, Hector Rivera and Ivan Villard, Sr.

Don Dodd was ordained as an elder on August 31.

Roy Sharp and Mike Cravens conducted a marriage seminar entitled

— 2003 —

"God's Blueprint for the Home" on September 19-21.

The Family Bible Bowl was held on October 11.

One of our deacons, Ron Cullom, died on October 13.

Our Eighth Annual South Florida Lectureship entitled "Written for Our Admonition" was on November 7-9.

Palm Beach Lakes assumed an overseeing role of Apologetics Press on November 6.

All Sunday morning Bible classes studied Christian Stewardship during the month of December.

Elders
Stan Bronson
Don Dodd
Joe Holland
Jerry Hopkins
Dan McLeod

Evangelists
Dan Jenkins
Ron Brackett
David Sproule, II

Deacons
David Brown
Novel Brown
Pete Brown
Mike Erickson
Tim Fry
Dan Fuller
Rick Hall
Gary Jenkins
Jeff Leslie
Greg Morris
Buzz Nelson
Harold Pack
Jerry Pittman
Phil Porter
Willie Smith
Scott Studer
Dirk Summerlot
Richard Watson

— 2003 —

Baptized (19)

Jan. 28	Rebecca Oakes
Feb. 02	Paul Whigham
Feb. 02	Matthew Hanna
Feb. 09	Steve Beaulieu
Feb. 12	David Noble
Mar. 12	Jamesena Cade
Apr. 29	Ralph Owens
May 11	Michael Trujillo
May 21	Richard Bowman Carr
June 02	Betty Yeoman
June 15	Wayne Alejandro Tamayo
July 15	Raymond & Margery Knisley
July 23	Katie Wagner
July 27	Sixtoria Phillips
Sep. 01	Jordan Beasley, Jr.
Sep. 17	Ashley Bowers
Oct. 12	Caila Buonadonna
Oct. 26	Nathaniel Echols

Restored (2)

Oct. 19	Marilyn Dixon
Nov. 05	Sylvester Jackson

Identified (36)

Jan. 08	Stephanie Colon
Jan. 12	Aaron & Leah Bronson
Jan. 12	Isolyn Dussard Sinclair
Jan. 12	Sylvia Dussard
Jan. 15	Michael & Julie Trujillo
Feb. 16	Lakiesha Hawkins
Feb. 16	Jewell Kircus
Mar. 02	Madalyn Hayward
Mar. 09	Glen & Josie Dawson
Mar. 16	Yvonne Golden
Mar. 16	Martha Hickson, Kelli, Kristi & Adria
Apr. 20	Don Wright
May 18	Andrew Layton
May 18	Derrick Banks
May 25	Judith Donovan
June 22	Norman & Marie Smedley
Aug. 24	Ricky & Leena Mack
Aug. 24	Rodney Robinson
Sep. 07	Cleave & Colleen Pamphile
Sep. 14	Tasha Bridgett
Nov. 16	George & Pat McMillan
Nov. 16	Richard, Agatha & Michael Ahlijah
Dec. 07	Shannon Thomas
Dec. 30	Wayne Tamayo

— 2003 —

Weddings (5)

June 21 Javier Trilla & Christie Ellis
June 28 Rob Shelt & April Dougherty
July 18 Chuck & Marisa Reeves
Oct. 07 Ryan Brackett & Aubrey Hickey
Oct. 18 Rodney Robinson & Jenny Anderson
Dec. 13 Kevin Weeks & Stephanie Hamlen

Births (9)

Jan. 16 Travis Michael Bates
Jan. 30 Mallory Rose Campbell
June 05 Haley Anita Hall
Aug. 28 Kayla Marie Bronson
Nov. 03 Joshua Michael Shelley
Nov. 16 Katelyn Renee Goodale
Nov. 29 Shayla Nicole Hawkins
Dec. 13 Shani Mack
Dec. 22 Emma Claire Reeves

Total Additions: 57 **274 Families; 498 Members**

— 2003 —

Died (8)
June 19 Aileen Belden
Aug. 03 Lucy Young
Sep. 12 Fran Reynolds
Oct. 04 Herman Smith
Oct. 13 Ron Cullom
Oct. 23 Ralph Owens
Nov. 04 Red Springer
Dec. 23 Bob DeVall

Moved Membership (9)
Jan. 19 Glena & Scott Maggart (Stuart)
Feb. 09 Mary Rudy (Suncoast)
Feb. 09 Patricia Eccles (Suncoast)
Feb. 16 Gloria Denson (Third Street)
June 15 Cindy, Sarah & Shelly Roberts (Suncoast)
Sep. 07 Wayne Tamayo (Palm City)

Moved Away (16)
Jan. 01 Mike Curington
Apr. 02 Shawn Mitchell
Apr. 02 Joel McLeod
May 10 Terri Flynn
June 08 Jennifer Peffer
June 29 Brianna Buckhalter
June 29 LaToya Ratliff
June 29 Billie Jo Sanderson
July 23 Rebecca Oakes
July 30 Ruby Hazlewood
Aug. 07 Brian, Jenni & Meredith Jones
Aug. 07 Judith Donovan
Sep. 28 Pam Smith
Oct. 05 Arlene Ruggles

Total Losses: 49   274 Families; 498 Members

— 2004 —

Our first Mission Sunday was on February 15. We collected $125,000 for missions this year on that one day.

Our spring Gospel Meeting was conducted on March 28-April 1 by Dave Miller from Apologetics Press in Montgomery, Alabama.

Our Twenty-Second Annual Ladies' Day was conducted on April 15. The speaker was Mattie Jackson, and the theme was "Lifting Others As You Climb."

A Mission Workshop conducted by Mark Blackwelder and Mark Hooper from Freed-Hardeman University was held on April 23-25.

Our annual Junior/Senior Banquet was held at the Double Tree Galleria in Fort Lauderdale. Nathaniel Nelson was selected King and won the award of best theme. Kelsey Ingram was selected Queen. Ivan Villard, Jr. was selected second runner-up to the King.

Rhonda Thompson conducted a Teachers' Workshop on May 22.

Cliff Boyd arrived in May to serve this summer as a preacher intern.

Two of our young men, Nathaniel Nelson and Taylor Reeves, served as summer interns at Apologetics Press in Montgomery, Alabama.

David Sproule took ten of our teens on a mission trip to Franklin, North Carolina on June 4-11.

Twenty-two of our teens accompanied David Sproule on a mission trip to Okeechobee on June 12-18.

Six new deacons were appointed on July 6: Aaron Bronson, Johnny Davis, Jeff Goodale, Paul Hensel, Bill Ingram, Jr. and Freddy Shelley.

Josh & Cara Blackmer and their son, Josiah, arrived on July 13. Josh will be working with our teens, and David will be doing more evangelism work.

David Sproule and Josh Blackmer took eight of our teens on a mission trip to Marsh Harbour, Bahamas on July 16-23.

An Evangelism Training for Youth conducted by Thaddeus Bruno and an Evangelism Training for Adults conducted by Dwayne Spradlin was held on August 6-7.

One of our deacons, Gary Jenkins, moved away on August 8.

Two very damaging hurricanes hit our area during September which caused us not to have worship services on two Sundays.

Two mission trips to Marsh Harbour in the Bahamas to help with their hurricane damage occurred on October 28-31 and November 4-7.

— 2004 —

The Ninth Annual South Florida Lectureship was held on November 12-14. The theme was "Stand in the Gap."

Elders
Stan Bronson
Don Dodd
Joe Holland
Jerry Hopkins
Dan McLeod

Evangelists
Dan Jenkins
Ron Brackett
David Sproule, II
Josh Blackmer

Deacons
Aaron Bronson
David Brown
Novel Brown
Pete Brown
Johnny Davis
Mike Erickson
Tim Fry
Dan Fuller
Jeff Goodale
Rick Hall
Paul Hensel
Bill Ingram, Jr.
Jeff Leslie
Greg Morris
Buzz Nelson
Harold Pack
Jerry Pittman
Phil Porter
Willie Smith
Freddy Shelley
Scott Studer
Dirk Summerlot
Richard Watson

— 2004 —

Baptized (8)
Feb. 18 Norma Pratt
Mar. 10 Rusty Mayne
Mar. 21 Jonathan Cousins
May 30 Larry Vernon Hill
June 05 Lee Hogue
June 30 Michael Archer
Sep. 15 Janice Morgan
Dec. 29 Jean Arthur

Identified (30)
Jan. 18 Sean & Kim Saunders
Jan. 25 Doug & Linda Drymon
Feb. 08 Larry & Nancy Beard
Feb. 15 Kizzy Torbert
Feb. 22 Tom Shiflett
Mar. 21 Bertha Sharpe Harrison
Apr. 11 Mary Meess
Apr. 18 Claudia, Casey & Kevan Allen
Apr. 28 Mrs. Lenelle Crowell
May 09 Mrs. Sara Norton
July 13 Josh & Cara Blackmer
Aug. 18 Patricia Green-Foxx
Aug. 22 Cynthia Parker
Aug. 22 Sherry Bulyca
Aug. 25 Sharon, Shandria, Steven, Mark, Marquise & Dominique Banks
Oct. 10 Allison Deem
Nov. 07 Rashard Jackson
Nov. 24 Kane & Fran Campbell
Nov. 26 Bonnie Barg

Restored (1)
July 07 Debbie Haymin

Weddings (3)
Jan. 02 Rusty Jordan & Heather Mayne
Oct. 26 Benjamin Pratt & Jamesena Cade
Dec. 09 Michael Archer & Jean Edwards

Births (9)
Mar. 06 Logan Michelle Brown
Mar. 15 Romaine Mayne, Jr.
Mar. 31 Gavin Saul Ellis
Aug. 10 Cody Richard Price
Aug. 12 Layla Marie Carter
Aug. 18 Raphael Bridgett
Aug. 23 Shai Madison McClain
Aug. 26 Devon Nathaniel Pamphile
Dec. 21 Kendyl Colon

Total Additions: 39

— 2004 —

Died (4)
Apr. 06 Rose Fifield
Apr. 25 Countess Waggoner
Sep. 18 Leon Johnson
Dec. 26 Ed Bashaw

Moved Away (24)
Jan. 18 Wayne Tamayo
Feb. 22 Anthony & Racquel Irvin
Apr. 18 Tim Heath
Apr. 25 Jerri, Cheri & Jenifer Flatt
June 05 Lloyd & Jalene Moody
June 27 Courtney Evans
July 11 Curtis Booth
Aug. 08 Gary, Jacqui, Lindsey & Daniel Jenkins
Aug. 08 Richard, Linda & Heather Longhenry
Sep. 26 Larry Hill
Oct. 30 Floyd Booth
Nov. 19 Carl & Madalyn Mack
Dec. 01 Benjamin & Jamesena Pratt

Moved Membership (9)
May 09 Shirley Holman (Third Street)
May 30 Robert, Angela & Jessica Fasig (Suncoast)
Aug. 08 Brad & Amanda Costello (Stuart)
Aug. 22 Debbie Haymin (Dodd Road)
Oct. 10 Rob & April Shelt (Stuart)

Total Losses: 56   **266 Families; 471 Members**

— 2005 —

Evangelism Sunday was on January 30, with a new Agape Program which was begun, with involvement encouraged for all members. New DVDs were distributed about Palm Beach Lakes.

The annual Sweetheart Banquet hosted by the Senior High for all those over age fifty-five or married for twenty-five years or more was on February 19. The theme was "One Night In Paris."

Mission Sunday was on February 27. Over $122,291 was collected for missions for this year.

Our spring Gospel Meeting was conducted on March 13-17 by David Lipe from Freed-Hardeman University. The theme was "Looking Unto Jesus."

Ladies' Day was on April 21 with Becky Blackmon of Fayetteville, GA as the speaker. The theme was "The Bread of Life."

Several members went on a mission trip to Trinidad on April 23-30.

A Junior/Senior High Bible Bowl was on Saturday, April 23.

The annual Junior/Senior Banquet was on Friday, May 13. Darin Summerlot was chosen King and Jelynne Carswell was first runner-up to the Queen and had best theme.

Cliff Boyd, David Milton and Nathaniel Nelson were our summer interns.

Greg Morris was ordained as an elder on May 22.

Josh Blackmer took some of the Senior High on a mission trip to Crestview, Florida on June 3-10. They went on another mission trip to Corinth, Mississippi on June 15-24.

Leadership Training Camp for Young Men was held on June 30-July 3.

Brackett Week at the Central Florida Bible Camp was on July 10-16.

There was a Leadership Training Camp for Young Women on July 21-24.

Dan McLeod resigned as elder on July 31 after serving five years.

There was an Evangelism Training for Youth conducted by Al Washington and a Leadership Forum conducted by Wendell & Mike Winkler on August 5-6.

Marian Holland resigned as one of the secretaries on August 1.

Several members went on a mission trip to Marsh Harbour on August 26-28.

Naomi Haltam began working as a secretary on September 19.

— 2005 —

The Tenth Annual South Florida Lectureship was on November 11-13. The Theme was "Respect For God's Word." Spanish classes were held for the first time. Speakers were Earl Edwards, Billy Davis, Jerry Jenkins, Don & Jane McWhorter, Dan Chambers, Dave Miller, Hardeman Nichols, Dan Jenkins, David Sproule, and Taylor Reeves. Singing was led by Dewight Lanham from Brentwood, TN.

Spiritual Enrichment Weekend was postponed to January because of hurricanes. Two services were cancelled because of the hurricanes. $17,500 in relief items were sent by Disaster Relief in Tennessee, which were distributed to the needy in this area.

The elders, deacons & preachers annual planning session was on November 25-27.

Another mission trip to Marsh Harbour was on November 25-27.

Elders	**Deacons**	**Deacons (cont.)**
Stan Bronson	Aaron Bronson	Bill Ingram, Jr.
Don Dodd	David Brown	Jeff Leslie
Joe Holland	Novel Brown	Buzz Nelson
Jerry Hopkins	Pete Brown	Harold Pack
Greg Morris	Johnny Davis	Jerry Pittman
	Mike Erickson	Phil Porter
Evangelists	Tim Fry	Freddy Shelley
Dan Jenkins	Dan Fuller	Willie Smith
Ron Brackett	Jeff Goodale	Scott Studer
David Sproule, II	Rick Hall	Dirk Summerlot
Josh Blackmer	Paul Hensel	Richard Watson

— 2005 —

Baptized (14)
Jan. 12 Brenda Weller
Jan. 15 Christopher Smith
Jan. 18 Ricky May
Apr. 17 Amanda Davenport
Apr. 22 Nelson & Karen Watts
May 08 Brayden Gilles (Trujillo)
June 01 Dianna Halenda
June 05 T.J. Hoelzer
July 03 Marjorie Ruiz
July 03 Tiffany Swisher
Aug. 09 Lucie Clemente
Aug. 28 Mary Dalsin
Oct. 18 Minor Hart

Restored (3)
June 05 Andrew Layton
July 17 Bettye J. King
July 31 George Harrison

Weddings (3)
Feb. 19 Jon Cousins & Christin Feeney
Aug. 19 Joe Quigley & Bonnie Barg
Dec. 17 David McLeod & Keila Villard

Births (7)
Mar. 13 Vivian Rose Blackmer
June 11 Austin Ryan Robinson
June 22 Ethan Brown
July 07 Brianna Makenzie Cousins
Sep. 13 Lamar Daniels (Torbert)
Oct. 14 Zachary James Bronson
Nov. 26 Jacob Andrew Heath

Identified (25)
Jan. 02 Mike & Tasha Ellis
Mar. 06 Phil & Noelle Daniele
Mar. 06 Mamie Beliech
Mar 27 Freddie Gadson
May 01 Denville & Dionne Wright
June 26 Betsy Merrill
Aug. 10 Trey Ingram
Aug. 14 Cam Crotts
Aug. 14 Shane Studer
Aug. 14 Kasey Vessel
Aug. 16 Eva Milsap
Aug. 19 Pat & Clayton Parnell
Sep. 04 Yvette Watts
Sep. 11 Naomi Haltam
Sep. 11 Pierre & Michalea Smith
Nov. 16 Denise Depino
Nov. 20 Andrea Edwards & Leroy Thompson
Dec. 11 David & Marie Thorpe

Total Additions: 42

— 2005 —

Died (7)

Apr. 16 Jerry Hoelzer
July 02 Anna Pacheco
July 03 Goldie Summerlot
Aug. 09 Rachel Cooper
Aug. 18 Hershel Knight
Sep. 25 Clara Mae Fort
Aug. 10 Mamie Beliech

Moved Away (32)

Feb. 13 Rose Williams
Mar. 06 Mary Meess
Mar. 27 Steve & Nohemi Rios
May 15 Rick & Linda Alexander
June 09 Tasha Bridgett
June 09 Valerie Humphries
June 09 Jeff & Kim Heath
June 20 Joe & Thelma Miller
July 10 Shoshanna Mickens
July 28 Blair & Lynette Brooker
July 31 Raymond & Margery Knisley
Aug. 07 Kelli & Kristi Hickson
Aug. 14 Chad & Christina Bates
Sep. 01 Lenny Langley
Sep. 07 Doug & Linda Drymon
Sep. 07 Jackie Stout
Nov. 20 Phil & Noelle Daniele
Dec. 13 David, Charlene & Ricky May
Dec. 30 John, Sue, Jon & T.J. Hoelzer

Moved Membership (10)

Apr. 03 Linda Martin (Dodd Road)
Apr. 03 Lois Soles (Dodd Road)
May 01 Connie West (Suncoast)
May 15 George & Pat McMillan (Boca/Delray)
Nov. 20 Pierre & Michalea Smith (Westside)
Dec. 18 Angel Fusco (Suncoast)
Dec. 18 Lucie Clemente (Suncoast)
Dec. 18 Rashard Jackson (Third Street)

Total Losses: 65   **261 Families; 443 Members**

— 2006 —

A booklet entitled "Heart, Soul, Mind, & Strength" was handed out to the congregation on January 29 to encourage every member at Palm Beach Lakes to become involved in the work of the church.

Mission Sunday was on February 19 with a contribution of $114,667.

Our spring Gospel Meeting was on March 5-9 with Hardeman Nichols as the speaker.

In March & April, our Wednesday evening classes watched "Searching for Truth" DVDs. Many were bought and handed out.

Ladies' Day entitled "M&M" was on April 20 with Becky Blackmon as the speaker.

An All-Church Work Day was held on April 29.

A Leadership Training Camp for Young Men was held on June 7-11.

A Leadership Training Camp for Young Women was on June 28-July 1.

Eight new deacons were appointed on July 9: Richard Ahlijah, Chuck Clark, Lance Collier, Mike Ellis, Dick Kelley, Cleave Pamphile, David Thorpe and Pete Zubriski.

Three of our deacons, Pete Brown, Harold Pack and Dirk Summerlot, resigned on February 5. Two of our deacons moved away: Freddy Shelley on October 22 and Cleave Pamphile on November 12.

An Evangelism Training for Youth was on August 4-5 with John Moore as the speaker.

In September, a Family News email started to be sent out to the congregation.

Our first Hispanic preacher, Douglas Alvarenga, his wife, Sandra, and daughter, Stephanie, arrived on November 1.

Our Eleventh Annual South Florida Lectureship entitled "Pearls from Proverbs" was held on November 10-12. The keynote speakers were Dan Jenkins, Robert Martin, Neal Pollard, and Sam Jones. Classes were conducted by Dale Jenkins, Jonathan Jenkins, Dwayne Spradlin, Rhonda Thompson, Dan Wheeler and Boyd Williams.

The annual EDP planning session was on November 17-18.

— 2006 —

Elders
Stan Bronson
Don Dodd
Joe Holland
Jerry Hopkins
Greg Morris

Evangelists
Dan Jenkins
Ron Brackett
David Sproule, II
Josh Blackmer
Douglas Alvarenga

Deacons
Richard Ahlijah
Aaron Bronson
David Brown
Novel Brown
Chuck Clark
Lance Collier
Johnny Davis
Mike Ellis
Mike Erickson
Tim Fry
Dan Fuller
Jeff Goodale
Rick Hall
Paul Hensel
Bill Ingram, Jr.
Dick Kelley
Jeff Leslie
Buzz Nelson
Jerry Pittman
Phil Porter
Willie Smith
Scott Studer
David Thorpe
Richard Watson
Pete Zubriski

— 2006 —

Baptized (14)
Apr. 09 Oliver & Leticia Hausler
June 06 Odell Simmons
June 26 Vita Chery
June 30 Winifred Patterson
July 01 Emilio Trejo
July 23 Peter Otero
Aug. 27 James Barber
Oct. 01 Austin Reeves
Oct. 07 Joe Quigley
Oct. 15 Nahum Villard
Oct. 22 Rachel Payne
Dec. 24 Larry Daniels
Dec. 31 Karlvellis Showers

Weddings (4)
Apr. 29 Minor Hart & Katie Feeney
June 16 Trey Ingram & Naomi Haltam
June 17 Jon Erickson & Cheri Kull
June 24 Shane Studer & Mindy Hensel

Births (3)
Apr. 23 Mackenzie Pamphile
June 13 Taylor Sue Price
June 16 Logan Thomas Carter

Identified (28)
Jan. 04 Susan Lupo & Mathea Obadiah
Jan. 04 Sara Senzamici
Jan. 22 Clarence Anthony, Jr.
Jan. 22 Kevin Perez
Mar. 12 Lawrence, Demetrius, Lawrence & Kayanna Richardson
Mar. 12 Gary & Michelle Franck
Mar. 15 Betty Sanders
Mar. 26 Amber Harrison
Apr. 02 Shirley Jones
Aug. 06 Natasha Campbell
Aug. 06 Ashley Francis
Aug. 06 Amanda Thompson
Aug. 13 Chris & Amy Erickson
Sep. 24 Linda Coe
Oct. 01 Jackie Stout
Oct. 08 Orlando, Lilly & Sabrina Lolo
Nov. 01 Douglas, Sandra & Stephanie Alvarenga
Dec. 17 Michael Barnes

Restored (1)
Sep. 10 Julio Vasquez

Total Additions: 43

— 2006 —

Died (11)
Jan. 18 Jewell Kircus
Feb. 02 Bob Davis
Apr. 16 Sue Clemans
Apr. 30 Oveda Hagans
May 09 Madella Scott
June 28 Harold Pack
July 07 Ruby Hilton
Aug. 10 Lois Soles
Aug. 16 Mary Katherine Knight
Sep. 26 Mary Blue Conner
Dec. 31 Irene Carver

Moved Away (29)
Feb. 28 Sherry Bulyca
Mar. 05 Frederick & Sebrina Key
Apr. 02 Nicole Campbell
Apr. 12 Oliver & Leticia Hausler
June 17 Jon Erickson
July 02 Martha Hickson family
July 02 Ricky & Leena Mack
Aug. 04 Denville & Dionne Wright
Aug. 04 Stephanie Colon
Aug. 15 George & Bertha Harrison
Aug. 15 Kizzy Torbert
Aug. 27 Lynn, Diane & Bethany Heath
Sep. 03 Ron Lupo, Susan & Mathea
Oct. 22 Freddy & Tori Shelley
Nov. 12 Cleave & Colleen Pamphile

Total Losses: 40   **264 Families; 426 Members**

— 2007 —

Stan Bronson resigned as elder for personal reasons on January 7.

A celebration was held in honor of Dan & Judie Jenkins for their twenty-five years with us.

Mission Sunday was on January 28 and $122,927 was collected.

The annual Sweetheart Banquet for members over fifty-five years old was hosted by the Senior High was on February 24. The theme was "A Night on the Spanish Main."

Our spring Gospel Meeting was on March 18-22 with Sam Jones from Freed-Hardeman University as the speaker.

Barry Hatcher was here for a Congregational Development Workshop on April 13-14.

Willie Smith was ordained as an elder on April 22.

Becky Blackmon was the speaker for the annual Ladies' Day on April 19. The theme was "Remodeling Your House."

A Creation/Evolution Seminar was conducted by Dr. Brad Harrub on May 4-6.

The Senior High Spring Banquet was held at the Palm Beach County Convention Center on May 18.

The Leadership Training Camp for Young Men was held on June 6-10.

The Leadership Training Camp for Young Women was held on June 13-17.

Josh Blackmer took a group of our teens on a mission trip to St. Petersburg, Florida on June 22-30.

Brackett Week at Central Florida Bible Camp for youth ages 10-18 was on July 15-21.

An Evangelistic Training for Youth conducted by Eric Gayle, Youth Director at Southwest church of Christ in Austin, Texas, was on August 3-5.

Troy & Andrea Spradlin left in August for Southwest School of Biblical Studies in Texas to prepare to do mission work in Paraguay in two years.

Robert Martin was here on October 7 for a report on the work he does in the Pacific Islands.

Scott Shanahan made a mission report on October 21.

Eight ladies from this congregation made a trip on October 12-14 to Marsh Harbour, Abaco, Bahamas to conduct a Ladies' Day.

Johnny Davis was ordained again as elder on September 23.

— 2007 —

Naomi Ingram resigned as one of the church secretaries the first of October after serving for two years. She and Trey moved to Jacksonville.

The Twelfth Annual South Florida Lectureship entitled "Increase My Faith" was held on November 9-11. The keynote speakers were Dan Jenkins, Phil Sanders, Chris Mitchell, Dave Miller and Al Washington. Classes were conducted by David Sproule, Kerry & Tommie Cain, Hardeman Nichols, Douglas Alvarenga and Bill Goodpasture.

The annual EDP planning session was on November 16-17.

Aaron Bronson, Mike Erickson and Pete Zubriski resigned as deacons at the end of the year.

Elders
Johnny Davis
Don Dodd
Joe Holland
Jerry Hopkins
Greg Morris
Willie Smith

Evangelists
Dan Jenkins
David Sproule, II
Ron Brackett
Josh Blackmer
Douglas Alvarenga

Deacons
Richard Ahlijah
David Brown
Novel Brown
Chuck Clark
Lance Collier
Mike Ellis
Tim Fry
Dan Fuller
Jeff Goodale
Rick Hall
Paul Hensel
Bill Ingram, Jr.
Dick Kelley
Jeff Leslie
Buzz Nelson
Jerry Pittman
Phil Porter
Scott Studer
David Thorpe
Richard Watson

— 2007 —

Baptized (18)
Jan. 14 Mary A. Jackson
Feb. 20 Sybil Carter
Mar. 18 Abdual Bootle
Mar. 22 Chad Brown
Mar. 28 Adelene Griffin
Apr. 08 Carolina Medina
Apr. 15 Gorman Ericksen
May 04 Maria Knitter
May 06 Shaina Boggan
June 04 Eva Fulton
June 10 Kelly Hall
June 17 Natalie (Medina) Villas
June 19 Dorothea Brown
July 10 Nirva Saintil
July 30 Mary W. Davis
Aug. 15 Esther Saintil
Aug. 26 Montekia Jones
Oct. 22 Rachel Payne

Identified (9)
Jan. 21 Bryan Schrager
Feb. 25 Bob & Angela Fasig
Feb. 25 Aren Elizee
May 27 Marie Watson
Sep. 09 Annie Faison
Sep. 16 Miles & Chrissy Davis
Sep. 30 Jessica Fasig

Restored (2)
Apr. 08 Nadia King
June 17 Jodi Brown

Weddings (3)
Apr. 05 David Miller & Jelynne Carswell
June 09 Hector Rene Rivera & Amanda Thompson
July 07 Ted Scheumann & Laura Leslie

Births (7)
Mar. 11 John H. Hawkins, Jr.
Mar. 16 Jake Tyler Ellis
Apr. 26 Dylan Matthew Campbell
May 22 Iziah Miller
Sep. 08 Trinity Franck
Sep. 14 Emma Reese Bronson
Dec. 27 Reagan Renee Studer

Total Additions: 29

— 2007 —

Died (4)
Jan. 16   Lucille Wright
Jan. 22   Emilio Trejo
Feb. 22   Don Hickerson
Sep. 02   Doris Seay

Moved Away (21)
Feb. 11   Ashley Francis
Feb. 18   Amber Harrison
Mar. 15   Kelly McClain
Mar. 15   Bryan & Beth Bonner
Apr. 08   Kenva Delancey
Apr. 29   Peter Williams
May 20   Beth Pittman
June 30   Shirley Jones
June 30   Ed & Ella Archer
July 22   Bryan Schrager
July 29   Peter Otero
Aug. 01   Troy & Andrea Spradlin
Aug. 26   Karlvellis Showers
Oct. 30   Kim Cooper
Oct. 06   Trey & Naomi Ingram
Oct. 21   Betty White
Oct. 21   Turkessa Femander

Moved Membership (4)
July 22   Brenda Weller (Third Street)
July 29   Rita Frederick (Haverhill)
Sep. 02   Kasey Vessel (Jog Road)
Oct. 21   Philip Girten (Jog Road)
Oct. 21   Emma Girten (Jog Road)

Total Losses: 39   **258 Families; 427 Members**

— 2008 —

Willie Smith resigned as elder on January 1.

One of our deacons, David Thorpe, placed membership at Jog Road on January 20.

Mission Sunday was on February 3, and $102,699.35 was given.

Our annual Sweetheart Banquet hosted by the teens for our older members was on February 9.

Amanda Rivera began working as one of our church secretaries on February 25.

Our spring Gospel Meeting was conducted by Phil Sanders on March 2-6. The theme of the meeting was "Why You Should Be a Christian."

On March 30, David Sproule began working with our teens again as Josh Blackmer began preparing to go to Paraguay next year as a missionary.

The speaker for our annual Ladies' Day on April 17 was Melanie Jenkins. The theme was "The Treasure of Contentment."

Ron Brackett left in May to become Director of Central Florida Bible Camp. Ron had been working at PBL since 1990, and he and Elizabeth had been members since 1978.

A Leadership Workshop was conducted on May 16-18 with J.J. Turner.

"Kick Start Your Summer" was held during June with different area preachers on Wednesday evenings. Vance Davis (Suncoast) spoke on June 4; Casey Haynes from Henderson, TN, who is being considered for Youth Leader here next year, spoke on June 11; Gale Nelson from Miami spoke on June 18; and Verlon Carroll from Lake Placid spoke on June 25.

David Sproule took a group of our teens on a mission trip to Fort Walton Beach, Florida on June 14-21.

Homecoming was held on July 4-6. Many of our former members attended, including Kerry Cain and Dewight Lanham.

Brackett/Jenkins week was on June 20-26 at Central Florida Bible Camp.

David Sproule took a group of our teens on a mission trip to Minnesota on August 2-8.

On August 15-16, a "Silencing of God Seminar" conducted by Dave Miller of Apologetics Press was held at P.B. Community College Auditorium.

Lindsey McPherson began working as one of the church secretaries on August 25.

— 2008 —

A new Tuesday morning Bible class began on September 9.

Palm Beach Lakes became the sponsoring congregation for Chris & Vicki Fry in Paraguay on October 1.

The Junior High hosted an "American Bandstand Dinner" for those over 50 on October 18.

Our Thirteenth Annual South Florida Lectureship, "The Joys of Christianity" based on Philippians, was held on November 7-9. Keynote speakers were Dan Jenkins, Dan Chambers, David Lipe and Rick Brumback. Breakout speakers were Allen Webster, Robert Martin, Greg Howard, James Mayo, Bill Burton, Traci Sproule and David Sproule. The song leader was Bill Burton.

Elders
Johnny Davis
Don Dodd
Joe Holland
Jerry Hopkins
Greg Morris

Evangelists
Dan Jenkins
David Sproule, II
Josh Blackmer
Douglas Alvarenga

Deacons
Richard Ahlijah
David Brown
Novel Brown
Chuck Clark
Lance Collier
Mike Ellis
Tim Fry
Dan Fuller
Jeff Goodale
Rick Hall
Paul Hensel
Bill Ingram, Jr.
Dick Kelley
Jeff Leslie
Buzz Nelson
Jerry Pittman
Phil Porter
Scott Studer
Richard Watson

— 2008 —

Baptized (18)
Feb. 13 Alvin Leaks, Jr.
Mar. 21 Ed Colditz
Apr. 20 Guadalupe Tipton
May 07 Sergio Rodriguez
May 28 Troy Petruzzi
June 15 Jennifer Romero
June 22 Billy McCormick
July 23 Abigail Saintil
July 23 Daniel Wagner
July 27 Ronnica Jenkins
July 27 Ziggy Ahlijah
Aug. 27 Ed Buonadonna
Sep. 10 Paul T. Lowe
Sep. 14 Elizabeth Carter
Sep. 16 Charlene Knowles
Sep. 19 Louis Osher
Dec. 29 Danielle Dixon

Identified (17)
Jan. 20 Gary, Jacqui & Daniel Jenkins
Mar. 19 Billie Cunningham
Mar. 23 Antonio & Kristina Velez
Apr. 20 Wayne & Margie Fortenberry
Apr. 20 Charleen Davis
July 02 Hollie Cheshier
July 06 Wesley Williams
July 23 Corey & Patti Bell
Aug. 24 Brent & Lindsey McPherson
Sep. 21 Michelle Manzi
Nov. 12 Erin Davis

Restored (5)
Mar. 19 Sharon Banks
Apr. 06 Terri Hahn
May 18 Cathy Seay
May 28 Loretta Holaday
Dec. 07 Keith Hatchett

Weddings (5)
Apr. 11 Ethan Bronson & Amanda Davenport
May 24 Nathaniel Nelson & Cindy Owens
June 07 Darin Summerlot & Jennifer Evans
June 14 Michael Rosenblum & Beth Pittman
July 30 Brent McPherson & Lindsey Jenkins

Births (3)
Apr. 27 Natalie Lynn Bronson
June 03 Connor Price Goodale
June 29 Kalen Michael Rivera

Total Additions: 40

— 2008 —

Died (7)
Jan. 17 Claudia Springer
Mar. 26 Don Wright
Apr. 01 Marilyn Dixon
Apr. 27 Dana Barnhouse
May 09 Dwight Clemans
Oct. 17 Ruby Johnson
Nov. 21 Marie Smedley

Moved Away (14)
Feb. 16 Lakiesha Hawkins
May 25 Ron & Elizabeth Brackett
June 28 Kelly Affron
July 16 Jodi Brown
July 28 Alvin & Judith Leaks
Aug. 20 Steven Reeves
Aug. 31 Ilene Edwards
Sep. 06 Saul & Becky Ellis
Oct. 26 Billy McCormick
Nov. 10 Carolina Medina & Natalie Villa

Moved Membership (21)
Jan. 20 David & Marie Thorpe (Jog Road)
July 16 Andrea Edwards (Third Street)
July 23 Ethan & Amanda Bronson (Haverhill)
July 23 Sara Bronson (Haverhill)
July 26 Maureen & Danny Machan (Jog Road)
Aug. 17 Charleen Davis (Suncoast)
Aug. 20 Minor & Katie Hart
Aug. 28 Sara Senzamici (Haverhill)
Sep. 07 Dan & Emily Richardson (Haverhill)
Nov. 09 Shane & Mindy Studer (Jupiter)
Nov. 23 Taylor Reeves (West Broward)
Dec. 07 Bob, Angela, Jessica & Nick Fasig (Jog Rd)

Total Losses: 47   **246 Families; 405 Members**

— 2009 —

Soldiers of Christ, a congregational Bible study on Sunday evenings, began in January.

January 25 was Mission Sunday and the total amount given on that day was $92,175.83.

One of our deacons, Richard Ahlijah, placed membership at Midway Road on February 15.

Our annual Sweetheart Banquet hosted by the teens for those over 55 was on February 21.

Our Cornerstone Groups were changed in February from five groups to four.

Our spring Gospel Meeting was conducted by Glenn Colley on March 1-3. The theme was "Back to Basics."

Kane Campbell, Victor Colage and Gary Jenkins were appointed as deacons on April 12.

Becky Blackmon was the speaker for our annual Ladies' Day on April 30. The theme was "Make Me A Barnabas."

Dale Jenkins was our speaker on May 3 for Super Sunday. The theme was "Celebrating the Family."

Casey & Hannah Haynes arrived on June 1 to begin working with our youth.

The speakers for Kick Start Your Summer were: Ron Brackett (June 3); Bill Weaver (June 10); Bill Goodpasture (June 17); Kerry Berkley (June 24).

On June 20, the congregation hosted a party for Dan & Judie Jenkins' Fiftieth Wedding Anniversary.

Mike Ellis resigned as deacon on June 21.

David Sproule took a group of our teens on a mission trip to Nashville, Tennessee on July 10-17.

Brackett/Jenkins week at Central Florida Bible Camp was on July 19-25.

Our Seventh Annual Evangelism Training for Youth was conducted by Kerry Williams on August 7-8.

Josh & Cara Blackmer and family left for Paraguay on August 30. Palm Beach Lakes would be their overseeing congregation while in the mission field.

Our second Super Sunday for this year was conducted by Phil Sanders on September 20.

— 2009 —

Scott Studer resigned as deacon on September 27.

Robert Martin gave a mission report on October 4.

The theme for our Fourteenth Annual South Florida Lectureship conducted on November 6-8 was "We Would See Jesus." Keynote speakers were Dan Jenkins, Dave Miller, Kyle Butt and Eric Lyons. Breakout speakers were Tommy Haynes, Troy Spradlin, Paul Sain, Mark Blackwelder, Deb Miller and Jim Day. The song leader was Gary Friedly.

Elders
Johnny Davis
Don Dodd
Joe Holland
Jerry Hopkins
Greg Morris

Evangelists
Dan Jenkins
David Sproule
Douglas Alvarenga

Deacons
David Brown
Novel Brown
Kane Campbell
Chuck Clark
Victor Colage
Lance Collier
Tim Fry
Dan Fuller
Jeff Goodale
Rick Hall
Paul Hensel
Bill Ingram, Jr.
Gary Jenkins
Dick Kelley
Jeff Leslie
Buzz Nelson
Jerry Pittman
Phil Porter
Richard Watson

— 2009 —

Baptized (11)
June 14 Joseph McKelton
July 13 Charles Espensen
Aug. 02 Sharon Casanova
Aug. 11 Kristen Fuller
Aug. 11 Lauren Fuller
Sep. 15 Tamela & Timothy Chappell
Sep. 28 Anthony Puckett
Oct. 01 Alexander Lane
Oct. 28 Betty Lavin
Dec. 31 Karl Duperat

Weddings (2)
June 20 Cam Crotts & Hollie Cheshier
Dec. 19 Brian Trejo & Kelly Affron

Identified (22)
Feb. 01 James, Floria, Brandon, Brian & Linda Allen
Feb. 15 Joycelyn Ables
Mar. 15 Carolina Medina & Natalie Villa
Mar. 29 Ellen Gager
June 01 Casey & Hannah Haynes
June 17 Robert Greninger
July 05 Stefan Holt
July 22 Jon & Cheri Erickson
July 22 Ken Worsham
Oct. 25 Les & Betty McQuinn
Nov. 18 Jorge Hernandez
Dec. 06 Don & Betty Matter
Dec. 09 Matthew Watson

Restored (4)
Mar. 29 Cornelius Brown
May 03 Danny Johnson
June 14 Paulette Cole
Dec. 20 Jermaine Smith

Total Additions: 37

— 2009 —

Died (4)
June 21   Dorothea Brown
Sep. 03   Lorine Johnson
Sep. 30   Samuel Quinn
Oct. 19   Evelyn Coleman

Moved Away (14)
Jan. 04   Billie Cunningham
Jan. 18   Johnny & Norma Young
Jan. 20   Michelle Manzi
Feb. 13   Mattie Davis
Mar. 04   Wayne & Margie Fortenberry
May 17   Hector & Amanda Rivera
Aug. 09   Quinntavias Smith
Sep. 24   Robert Lupo
Sep. 29   Josh & Cara Blackmer
Oct. 25   Maria Knitter

Moved Membership (7)
Feb. 15   Richard Ahlijah family (4)
          (Midway Road)
Aug. 09   Javier & Christie Trilla
          (Jupiter/Tequesta)
Dec. 13   Stan Bronson (Boca Raton)

Total Losses: 30   **236 Families; 392 Members**

— 2010 —

Singing classes resumed at 5:30 p.m. on Sunday, January 10.

There was a "going away" party for Troy and Andrea Spradlin on Sunday, January 24, as they left for Paraguay.

Mission Sunday was on January 31. Total amount given was 121,558.73.

There was a new member breakfast on Saturday, February 20.

Casey Haynes took our teen group to the Challenge Youth Conference meeting in Gatlinburg, Tennessee on Friday-Sunday, February 26-28.

Our Gospel Meeting was on March 7-10 with Tommy Haynes from Moore, Oklahoma. The theme was "Power to Become."

Our speaker for Ladies' Day on Thursday, April 15 was Roberta Edwards from Port au Prince, Haiti. We had our largest attendance with 330 present. The topic was "His Eye Is on the Sparrow."

Friends and Family Day was on May 16 with the theme of "That's the Power of Love."

"Kick Start Your Summer" Series on Wednesday evenings began on June 2. The theme of the lessons was "I Need Thee Every Hour." This year's speakers were Tracy Moore (Vero Beach), Ernest Mackifield, Ricky Kimble (Sixth Street in Pompano), and Dan Wheeler (Concord Street in Orlando)

Our first Vacation Bible School in many years was conducted Sunday-Wednesday, June 13-16 with the theme "Rise & Shine for Jesus."

The Leadership Training Camp for Young Men and Young Women was on June 23-27.

Casey Haynes took a group of our teens on a mission trip to Ulysses, Kansas on July 8-16.

Brackett/Jenkins Week at Central Florida Bible Camp was July 25-31.

Our Eighth Annual Evangelism Training for Youth was on August 6-7. The keynote speaker was Chuck Morris from Jackson, Tennessee. Speakers for the classes were Ron Brackett; Ray Gosa, Jr.; James Mayo; Bill Weaver; Dan Fuller; and David Sproule.

After serving as one of our church secretaries for 2 years, Lindsey McPherson resigned and moved to Tennessee on August 1.

Cindy Nelson began working in the office on Monday, August 2 as one of our secretaries.

An announcement was made on Sunday, September 19 that the Hispanic group that has been meeting in our building since 2003 would merge with the Jog Road congregation and begin meeting in their building on Octo-

— 2010 —

ber 3. Douglas Alvarenga will begin raising support to begin a mission work in San Juan, Argentina next year.

Sam Jones was the speaker for "A Perfect Day" Super Sunday on October 10.

The elders, deacons and preachers met for their annual planning session on Friday-Saturday, October 15-16.

About sixty members attended Spiritual Enrichment Weekend at Central Florida Bible Camp on October 22-24.

Chris Fry gave his final report on his six-year work in Paraguay on Sunday, October 31. He and his family are returning to the States in March 2011.

Our Fifteenth Annual South Florida Lectureship, entitled "We Would See Jesus, the Son of Man," was held on Friday-Sunday, November 5-7. Keynote speakers were Jay Lockhart from Benton, KY; David Powell from Henderson, TN; Jerry Houston from Rochester, NY; and Jeff Jenkins from Lewisville, TN. Breakout class teachers not already listed were Mike Winkler from Madison, AL; Gary Hampton from Knoxville, TN; Randall Hunter from Stuart, FL; Vance Davis, Suncoast; Rhonda Thompson, Henderson, TN; Benny Santiago, Jog Road; and Dan Jenkins. Singing was led by Gary Friedly.

Kane Campbell resigned as deacon on November 21.

Our new and improved website was revealed to the congregation on December 12, 2010, after being hacked on October 10.

Elders	Deacons	Deacons (cont.)
Johnny Davis	David Brown	Paul Hensel
Don Dodd	Novel Brown	Bill Ingram, Jr.
Joe Holland	Chuck Clark	Gary Jenkins
Jerry Hopkins	Victor Colage	Dick Kelley
Greg Morris	Lance Collier	Jeff Leslie
	Tim Fry	Buzz Nelson
Evangelists	Dan Fuller	Jerry Pittman
Dan Jenkins	Jeff Goodale	Phil Porter
David Sproule	Rick Hall	Richard Watson
Douglas Alvarenga		

— 2010 —

Baptized (17)
Jan. 31 Precious Simon
Mar. 25 Marcia Clough-Moss
Apr. 11 Kaitlyn Donahue
Apr. 19 Regina Paul
Apr. 29 Beau Boshers
May 05 Rodney Harris
June 27 Rodney Robinson
Aug. 02 Norman Miller
Aug. 04 Ricky Smith
Aug. 04 Nikki Revoli
July 30 Selvin Mills (at camp)
July 30 Jessica Gibbins (at camp)
Sep. 19 Nancy Colaprete
Sep. 26 Ana Rodrigues
Oct. 03 Debbie Boshers
Oct. 29 Mary Coombs
Nov. 26 Warren Porter

Weddings (4)
June 05 Chuck Espensen & Casey Byerly
June 09 Stephen Beliech & Carolina Contreras
June 11 Beau Boshers & Debbie Bennett
June 19 Dirk Summerlot & Elizabeth Trejo

Births (1)
Feb. 17 Elias Jayvyn Davis

Identified (37)
Jan. 31 Jeremy Maloney
Feb. 14 Woodline Jadis
Feb. 28 Francinia, Felicia & Rakita Jackson
May 19 Gabriel & Jennifer Chaffin
May 23 Sherrick, Mary, Brandon & Chris Thomas
May 30 John Tsikata
July 28 Nathaniel & Cindy Nelson
Aug. 01 Betty White
Aug. 01 Turkessa Femander
Aug. 22 Abby Crager
Aug. 29 Westley, Lillie & DJ Cherrelus
Sep. 01 Jon, Jenny, Jessica & Jon Jordan
Sep. 05 Blake & Dana Gastelum
Sep. 05 Drew Humphries
Sep. 05 Kirk & Mandy Crews
Sep. 19 Kevin & Michele Rebal
Sep. 26 Lennie Langley
Nov. 21 Rebecca McCorkle
Nov. 21 Harrison Carter
Dec. 19 Lawrence & Julie Williams & Brianna Solis

Restored (5)
June 27 Iva Ardoin
July 25 Jim & Robin Davis
Sep. 26 Diane Catanzaro
Oct. 03 Lynne Lawton

Total Additions: 59

— 2010 —

Died (2)
Mar. 11 James Barber
June 11 Marion Sherrod

Moved Away (19)
Mar. 14 Matt Ellis
Apr. 07 Kyle Milton
June 24 Ricky May
July 04 Sixtoria Phillips
Aug. 01 Carolina Medina & Natalie Villa
Aug. 04 Brent & Lindsey McPherson
Sep. 01 Francina, Rakita & Felicia Jackson
Sep. 26 Blake & Dana Gastelum
Sep. 26 Abby Crager
Nov. 28 Cynthia Chow
Dec. 19 Jelynne Miller
Dec. 28 Drew Humphries
Dec. 28 Norman Miller
Dec. 29 Roger Mars

Moved Membership (7)
Mar. 14 Chris Erickson (Jupiter/Tequesta)
Apr. 07 Aaron & Leah Bronson (Haverhill)
June 24 Kim Worthington (Jupiter/Tequesta)
Aug. 29 Woodeline Jadis (Suncoast)
Sep. 26 Hector & Ele Rivera (Jog Road)

Total Losses: 41   **255 Families; 416 Members**

— 2011 —

A New Members' Breakfast was held on Saturday, January 29 for everyone becoming members at Palm Beach Lakes last year, either by being baptized, placing membership or being restored.

Mission Sunday was on Sunday, January, 30. A total of $113,788.90 was given.

Dan Fuller was ordained as an elder on Sunday, February 27.

Our Gospel Meeting was on March 6-9 with Sam Jones from Henderson, Tennessee as the speaker. The theme of the meeting was "If This Was the Only Book I Ever Followed."

Richard Watson resigned as a deacon on Sunday, April 10 for personal reasons.

Don & Carol Dodd moved to Soddy Daisy, Tennessee on April 14 to be with their children. Don served as deacon from February 6, 1983 until he was ordained as an elder on August 31, 2003, serving faithfully for 8 years.

Our annual Ladies' Day was on Thursday, April 14 with Cindy Colley from Huntsville, Alabama as the speaker. Her topic was "He Is LORD of Lords."

Tom Holland was here on Saturday-Sunday, May 7-8 for lessons on "Building Up the Church in the Twenty-First Century" and "The Joy of Being a Christian."

Phil Porter took a group of members on a mission trip to Paraguay in June.

Vacation Bible School was on Sunday-Wednesday, June 19-22 with classes for all ages.

Greg Morris moved to Memphis, Tennessee on June 30, Michelle to follow later this year. Greg had served as deacon from March 6, 1988 to May 22, 2005, and as elder from May 22, 2005 until moving away on June 30, 2011.

Douglas & Sandra Alvarenga moved to Omaha, Nebraska in June to prepare to raise funds to begin a mission work in San Juan, Argentina within the next eighteen months.

Brackett/Jenkins week was on July 24-30 at Central Florida Bible Camp.

Our Ninth Evangelism Training for Youth was on August 5-7 with Lonnie Jones as speaker.

Casey & Hannah Haynes moved back to Oklahoma on October 31.

Our Sixteenth Annual South Florida Lectureship, "Heaven's Home-

— 2011 —

Improvement Workshop," was held on November 3-6. Speakers included Jerrie Barber (Nashville, TN); Glenn Colley (Huntsville, AL); Chris Fry (Dyersburg, TN); Stan Mitchell (Henderson, TN); Eric Owens (Atlanta, GA); Roy Sharp (Henderson, TN); Bill Weaver (Orlando, FL); and Dan Winkler (Huntington, TN).

Elders
Johnny Davis
Dan Fuller
Joe Holland
Jerry Hopkins

Evangelists
Dan Jenkins
David Sproule

Deacons
David Brown
Novel Brown
Chuck Clark
Victor Colage
Lance Collier
Tim Fry
Jeff Goodale
Rick Hall
Paul Hensel
Bill Ingram, Jr.
Gary Jenkins
Dick Kelley
Jeff Leslie
Buzz Nelson
Jerry Pittman
Phil Porter

— 2011 —

Baptized (26)

Jan. 02	Shelton Howell
Feb. 02	Stacy Hey
Feb. 13	Phalin Mitchell
Feb. 13	Derrek Johnson
Mar. 09	Robert Paulin
Mar. 09	Scarlett Starnes
Mar. 23	Jason & Melanie Jerusalem
Apr. 04	Lynne Jorgensen
May 22	Ronald & Denise Mills
May 29	Brittany Croft
June 05	Austin Metzkes
June 29	Barbara Williams
July 03	Cassie Lavender (Higbee)
July 10	Shannon Lopez
July 28	David Payne, II
Aug. 07	Brianna Solis (Williams)
Aug. 28	Cortneia Lindsey
Sep. 17	Rick Price
Sep. 18	Samuel Lanier
Sep. 28	Givenson & Japhna Benel
Oct. 26	Grant Fuller
Nov. 20	Nicholas Pietro
Dec. 25	Tyrone Toson

Restored (5)

Feb. 09	Lisa Eutsey
Feb. 13	Lester Galloway
Apr. 03	Leesa Schenk
June 05	Tammy Matsuo
Aug. 14	Amy Erickson

Identified (36)

Feb. 05	Ally Alberga
Feb. 13	Sam & Peggy Simpkins
Feb. 20	Adam Seal
Apr. 20	Paul, Lisa & Meagan Metzkes
Apr. 24	Jason Chavez
May 22	Kahla King
May 22	Maurine Reed
May 22	Bob & Jennifer Higbee
June 12	John, Sue & Jon Hoelzer
July 03	Christopher Thompson
July 10	Namdidie, Ekaette & Ekemini Ikon
July 10	Brian & Summer Mayerbach
Aug. 07	Danielle Harlee
Aug. 21	Taylor Reeves
Aug. 21	Edward Gager
Aug. 28	Jessica Duke
Aug. 28	Alex & Emily Lane
Oct. 31	Earl & Louise Brown
Nov. 20	Cherylann Wineinger
Nov. 27	Charles Hayes
Dec. 04	Regina Mayne
Dec. 11	Ross, Robin & Kailee Stone
Dec. 18	Harriet Morris

Weddings (2)

June 25	Matthew Watson & Julie Leslie
Aug. 10	Christopher Thompson & Brittany Croft

Total Additions: 67

— 2011 —

Births (5)
Jan. 26 Melanie Elise Weeks
Jan. 27 Elena Katherine Carter
June 29 Carter Thomas Crotts
July 13 Kipton Elijah Chaffin
Sep. 13 Malakai Chavez

Died (4)
Feb. 11 Floria Allen
Aug. 11 Bob Tooker
Oct. 12 Maxine Jacoby
Oct. 28 Madalyn Hayward

Moved Away (26)
Jan. 27 Rebecca McCorkle
Mar. 29 Westley, Lillie & DJ Cherrelus
Apr. 06 Ken & Martie Veverka
Apr. 14 Don & Carol Dodd
Apr. 22 Sammy Jackson
May 15 Selvin Mills
May 22 John Tsikata
June 01 Douglas & Sandra Alvarenga
June 19 Kevin & Michele Rebal
June 22 Quinntel Smith
June 30 Greg & Michelle Morris
July 17 Robert Greninger
Oct. 04 Barbara Williams
Oct. 09 Beau & Debbie Boshers
Oct. 30 Casey & Hannah Haynes
Dec. 15 Jason & Melanie Jerusalem

Moved Membership (4)
Oct. 02 Miles & Chrissie Davis (Stuart)
Oct. 09 Casey Espensen (Stuart)
Dec. 11 Tasha Bridgett (Jog Road)

Total Losses: 37   **273 Families; 450 Members**

— 2012 —

Eric Lyons from Apologetics Press was here on January 27-29 to speak to our teens about Creation, Evolution and Dinosaurs.

Mission Sunday was on January 29, and $107,298.60 was given.

Our New Members' Breakfast was held on Saturday, February 4.

Phil Porter was ordained as an elder on February 12.

A Congregational Singing Workshop was conducted on February 17-18 by Gary Friedly.

Our Gospel Meeting was on March 4-7 with Neal Pollard from Denver, Colorado as the speaker. The theme of the meeting was "The Essentials."

A Leadership Training Course, especially for men, was held at 5:00 p.m. from March 11 until May 20.

Our Thirtieth Annual Ladies' Day was on Thursday, April 19 with Kathy Haynes from Moore, Oklahoma as the speaker. Her topic was "Striving to Win."

Friends and Family Day was on May 20. The theme was "In the Shelter of His Wings."

One of our deacons, Bill Ingram, Jr., resigned on June 3.

The theme for our Kick Start Your Summer Series in June was "Oh, How I Love Jesus."

Vacation Bible School was on June 17-20. The theme was "Christian Academy: Training Superheroes for God."

A Leadership Training Camp for Young Men and Young Women was conducted on June 27-30.

Brackett/Jenkins Week at Central Florida Bible Camp was on July 22-28.

Dan & Judie Jenkins went to Fiji to work with Robert Martin on a mission trip on July 25-August 14.

Seven new deacons were appointed on July 29: Michael Archer, Kirk Crews, Jim Davis, Michael Erickson, Bob Higbee, Paul Metzkes and Kevin Weeks.

Super Sunday with Billy Smith from Henderson, Tennessee was on September 16. The theme was "Victory in Jesus."

September 21-23 was our first effort to affix 100,000 labels to House-to-House/Heart-to-Heart newsletters, which was finished in four hours.

A Teacher Workshop was conducted on Saturday, October 20 and 27

— 2012 —

for a new children's Bible class program to begin in January 2013.

Our Seventeenth Annual South Florida Lectureship, "I Love the Church of Christ Because...," was held on November 8-11. Speakers included Mark Blackwelder (Henderson, TN); David Lipe (Baxter, TN); James Miller (Freeport, Grand Bahamas); Dan & Grace Wheeler (Orlando, FL); and Dan Winkler (Huntingdon, TN).

Elders
Johnny Davis
Dan Fuller
Joe Holland
Jerry Hopkins
Phil Porter

Evangelists
Dan Jenkins
David Sproule, II

Deacons
Mike Archer
David Brown
Novel Brown
Chuck Clark
Victor Colage
Lance Collier
Kirk Crews
Jim Davis
Mike Erickson
Tim Fry
Jeff Goodale
Rick Hall
Paul Hensel
Bob Higbee
Gary Jenkins
Dick Kelley
Jeff Leslie
Paul Metzkes
Buzz Nelson
Jerry Pittman
Kevin Weeks

— 2012 —

Baptized (15)
Feb. 12   Clayton Trujillo
Feb. 15   Dadlanie Vincent
Mar. 05   Juliette Mauvais
Apr. 30   Patrick Waller
May 20   Madison Herrera
June 13   Christene Bean
July 01   Katie Sproule
July 27   Whitney Williams (at camp)
July 27   John Vargas (at camp)
Sep. 05   Justilien Honore
Sep. 05   Astrid Beliech
Sep. 09   Carla Owens
Nov. 04   Sabrina Pietro
Nov. 11   Tyler Williams
Nov. 25   Tia Spizziro

Restored (2)
Jan. 01   Roy Ike Crocker
Nov. 25   Jimmie Banks

Weddings (3)
May 05   Taylor Reeves & Natalie Smith
Sep. 16   Justilien Honore & Adelene Griffin
Oct. 06   Jon Hoelzer & Priscilla Diaz

Births (1)
Nov. 06   Amni Lee Chavez

Identified (29)
Feb. 19   Julio, Flo, Julio, III & Arianna Aristy
Feb. 22   Brian & Tammy Rayfield
Mar. 11   Barbara Williams
Mar. 11   Adrienne Gadson
Apr. 04   Matt Ellis
Apr. 08   Dorothy Savage
Apr. 22   David & Marie Thorpe
Apr. 29   Adrienne Gadson
May 13   Natalie Reeves
June 10   Ted & Karen Friesner
July 08   Jim & Jo Ann Rogers
July 08   Vincent & Lovella Rogers
Aug. 12   David & Sally Roff
Sep. 23   Carolyn Preston
Sep. 23   Teresa Williams
Sep. 23   Kendra & Kirstin Voet
Oct. 14   Joel & Cherilyn Basrally
Nov. 11   Mark Lester

Total Additions: 46

— 2012 —

Died (5)
Jan. 22 Nora Lee Meinschein
Feb. 06 Wayne Fortenberry
May 15 Nirva Saintil
June 17 Louise Brown
Dec. 06 Sara Crocker

Moved Away (8)
Jan. 04 Stephanie Bustos
Jan. 29 Paul Lowe
Mar. 25 Mike Barnes
Aug. 26 Barbara Williams
Sep. 04 John Vargas
Sep. 04 Patrick Waller
Sep. 26 Robert Paulin
Dec. 30 Stacy Hey

Moved Membership (3)
Aug. 22 Yvonne Golden (Jog Road)
Aug. 22 Yvette Watts & Phalin Mitchell (Jog Road)

Total Losses: 27   **275 Families; 457 Members**

— 2013 —

A new Bible class program for children Age 3 thru Grade 5 began on January 6 called "Stepping into the Bible."

Josh Blackmer made a mission report on Sunday, January 13.

Mission Sunday was on January 27 with $119,289 given this day.

A New Members' Breakfast for all who were baptized or placed membership last year was held on February 16.

The Sweetheart Banquet hosted by the Junior High was on February 23.

Our Gospel Meeting was on March 3-6 with Dan Winkler as the speaker. The subject was "The Freedom of Forgiveness." The lunch subject was "From the Lips of a Dying Savior."

Our annual Ladies' Day was on April 18 with Becky Blackmon of Waco, Texas as the speaker. The subject was "Choosing to Serve."

Jud Davis, from Freed-Hardeman University, spoke on "Keeping the Faith" on Sunday, April 21.

Evangelism Training for Youth was held on May 3-4 with Casey Haynes as the speaker. The subject was "Our Youth, Their Families & the Church."

Scott Shanahan gave a mission report on Sunday, May 19.

One of our deacons, Kirk Crews, moved away on May 31.

Vacation Bible School was conducted on June 16-19 with the theme "Christian Academy: The Battle Belongs to the Lord."

Troy Spradlin gave a mission report on June 9.

The theme for our "Kick Start Your Summer" series was "Amazing Grace, How Sweet the Sound." Brad Smith, from West Broward, began with "I Once Was Lost, But Now I'm Found" on June 5. Douglas Alvarenga spoke on June 12 on "Thru Many Dangers, Toils, & Snares." Bruce Daugherty, from Daytona, spoke on June 26 on "The Lord Has Promised Good to Me." And Kevin Patterson, from Sebring, spoke on July 3 on "When We've Been There Ten Thousand Years."

Our annual Leadership Training Camp for Young Men and Young Women was held on June 26-30.

Brackett/Jenkins Week at Central Florida Bible Camp was July 21-27.

A seminar by Dave Miller entitled "Islam, the Quran & New Testament Christianity" was held on September 20-22.

Robert Martin gave a mission report on October 6.

— 2013 —

Spiritual Enrichment Weekend at Central Florida Bible Camp was on October 11-13.

Our Eighteenth Annual South Florida Lectureship was on November 7-10. The theme was "God Has Spoken." Keynote Speakers were Dan Jenkins, Jody Apple, Eric Owens and Jesse Robertson. Breakout classes were taught by Brent Kercheville, Jeff Miller, Bill & Lori Boyd, David Sproule, and various PBL teachers. Gary Friedly led the singing at all sessions.

Mauricio Yegros gave a mission report on December 8.

Because of the holiday, our midweek Bible study and the New Year's Eve service and party were held on Thursday instead of Wednesday.

Elders
Johnny Davis
Dan Fuller
Joe Holland
Jerry Hopkins
Phil Porter

Evangelists
Dan Jenkins
David Sproule

Deacons
Mike Archer
David Brown
Novel Brown
Chuck Clark
Victor Colage
Lance Collier
Jim Davis
Mike Erickson
Tim Fry
Jeff Goodale
Rick Hall
Paul Hensel
Bob Higbee
Gary Jenkins
Dick Kelley
Jeff Leslie
Paul Metzkes
Buzz Nelson
Jerry Pittman
Kevin Weeks

— 2013 —

Baptized (8)
Jan. 12   Kaylani Carmona
Feb. 20   Leslie Sawyer
Mar. 13   Aryanna Duhl
May 20   Austin Williams
July 24   Anthony Stinnett (at camp)
Oct. 23   Andrea Garcia
Nov. 13   Gloria Boyd
Dec. 25   Steven (Andy) Griffiths

Births (1)
Aug. 07   Roderick Louis McLeod

Identified (9)
Feb. 03   Louise Phillips
Feb. 03   Sandy Mann
Feb. 03   Marjorie Ruiz-Carmona & Kaylani
Feb. 17   Wallace Jones
Feb. 24   Zula McLeod Garrett
Mar. 17   Major & Allison Roman
Sep. 29   Dianne Frye

Restored (2)
Feb. 24   Deboria Walker
June 30   Selvin Mills

Weddings (5)
May 25   Matt Ellis & Olivia Swearingen
May 29   David Farrington & Stacy Hall
June 17   Daniel Simons & Allison Price
Nov. 27   Brent Leslie & Andrea Garcia
Dec. 14   Ben Harriott & Joycelyn Ables

Total Additions: 19

— 2013 —

Died (2)
June 10 Betty Yeoman
Oct. 15 Sara Norton

Moved Away (22)
Feb. 02 Gloria Dixon
Apr. 15 Gabriel & Jennifer Chaffin
May 19 Lou Osher
May 31 Kirk & Mendy Crews
May 31 Nahum Villard
May 31 David & Sally Roff
May 31 Corey & Patty Bell
May 31 Ronnica Jenkins
June 12 Stacy Hall Farrington
June 16 Matthew & Julie Watson
June 17 Allison Price Simons
Sep. 01 Brian & Tammy Rayfield
Sep. 15 Kayanna Richardson
Oct. 06 Joel & Cherilyn Basrally
Nov. 17 Selvin Mills

Total Losses: 37   **269 Families; 415 Members**

— 2014 —

Mission Sunday was on January 26, and $112,487.21 was collected.

It was announced on February 16 that Josh Blackmer would be returning from Paraguay in September to work with this congregation as an evangelist doing Family/Youth Work.

Our Gospel Meeting was on March 9-12 with David Lipe speaking on "Finally ... Some Good News."

Ladies' Day was on April 17 with Kathy Pollard of Denver, Colorado as the speaker. The topic was "The Bride of Christ."

Troy Spradlin gave a mission report on Sunday, April 27.

Kyle Butt from Apologetics Press was the speaker for Eternity Training for Youth on May 2-4.

"Coming Home" Sunday was on May 18. Hundreds of cards were sent to former members encouraging them to return to the church. Six former members were restored.

"Kick Start Your Summer" Series, with the theme of "Count Your Blessings," began on June 4 with Lawrence Gilmore speaking on "You Have God's Promises." Terry Casey from West Broward spoke on June 11 on "You Have God's Peace." James Mayo from Jupiter/Tequesta spoke on June 25 on "You Have God's People." Kevin Patterson from Sebring spoke on July 2 on "You Have God's Providence."

Vacation Bible School with the theme of "God's Creation" was on Thursday-Friday, June 11-13.

Paul & Lisa Metzkes took seven of our young people on a mission trip to Roswell, Georgia on June 20-27.

Leadership Training Camp for Young Men and Young Women was on July 9-13.

Jenkins week at Central Florida Bible Camp was on July 20-26, followed by Upward Bound on July 26-30.

Jeff Miller conducted a Science vs. Evolution Seminar entitled "Evolution Is Unscientific" on August 29-31.

Joey Treat made a mission report on Sunday, September 21.

Josh & Cara Blackmer returned from Paraguay to work with Family/Youth on October 5.

Spiritual Enrichment Weekend at CFBC was on October 10-12 with about fifty of our members attending.

Paul Hensel resigned as a deacon on November 9.

— 2014 —

Our Nineteenth Annual South Florida Lectureship was on November 6-9. The subject was "Part of the Family." Keynote speakers were Dan Jenkins, Jonathan Jenkins, Dale Jenkins and Jeff Jenkins. Breakout speakers were Andrew Jenkins, Mona Jenkins and Gary Jenkins.

Our Wednesday Midweek Bible Study for December 24 was rescheduled for Tuesday, December 23 because of the holiday.

Elders
Johnny Davis
Dan Fuller
Joe Holland
Jerry Hopkins
Phil Porter

Evangelists
Dan Jenkins
David Sproule
Josh Blackmer

Deacons
Mike Archer
David Brown
Novel Brown
Chuck Clark
Victor Colage
Lance Collier
Jim Davis
Mike Erickson
Tim Fry
Jeff Goodale
Rick Hall
Bob Higbee
Gary Jenkins
Dick Kelley
Jeff Leslie
Paul Metzkes
Buzz Nelson
Jerry Pittman
Kevin Weeks

— 2014 —

Baptized (15)
Jan. 12 Grace Hackshaw
Jan. 12 Carmen Ruckman
Feb. 02 Eldra Judge
Feb. 09 Rodney Woods
Feb. 16 Anthony Reed
Feb. 16 Kelly Sproule
Mar. 02 Tomekea Forde
Mar. 10 Cody Penzera
Mar. 15 Angie McNicol
Mar. 28 Valerie Houghtaling
Apr. 01 Ophelia Holmes
Apr. 19 Chris Manning
Apr. 20 Phyiona Patterson
Sep. 17 Carol Hardman
Oct. 05 Michael Fox

Identified (19)
Jan. 12 Richard Lerro
Mar. 15 John McNicol
Mar. 23 Carolina Medina
Mar. 30 Ben Harriett
Apr. 02 Judy Lerro
May 18 Daniel Swayne
July 13 Luther Robinson
July 20 Cornelius & Andrea Henderson, Gabrielle Newby
July 27 Monica Morando
Aug. 10 Paul & Nellie Batitsky
Aug. 10 Lana Smith
Aug. 31 Daniel & Daisy Lord
Sep. 28 Ken & Connie Tipton
Nov. 09 Jaqua' Lewis

Restored (7)
Apr. 23 Angela Freeman
May 02 Amy (Newman) Rosado
May 18 Mike Damron
May 18 Hazel Hackshaw
May 18 Valerie MacDougal
June 01 Jordan Beasley
June 22 Helen Chapman

Weddings (3)
Jan. 11 Harrison Carter & Danielle Harley
May 01 David Santana & Jessica Jordan
June 21 Ivan Villard, Jr. & Amber Pittman

Births (3)
Jan. 01 Caleb Beliech
Aug. 07 Griffin Goodale
Nov. 13 Maddon Cole Reeves

Total Additions: 41

— 2014 —

Died (8)

Jan. 10   James Allen
Feb. 08   Donna Armstrong
June 14   Karen Watts
July 17   Gladys Jackson
July 20   Margie Fortenberry
Aug. 01   Angie McNicol
Oct. 12   Lennie Langley
Nov. 18   Walter Arthur

Moved Membership (5)

Feb. 05   Ray Seay (Stuart)
June 22   Kendra & Kirstin Voet
          (Jog Rd)
Aug. 03   Nikki Revoli (Suncoast)
Aug. 31   Stephanie Hensel
          (Jupiter/Tequesta)

Moved Away (24)

Mar. 02   Brittney Humphries
Mar. 13   Jack & Dee Jaggers
Apr. 02   Ronald & Denise Mills
May 01   Jon & Cheri Erickson
May 01   Cody Penzera
May 25   Mark Lester
June 07   Darlene Smith
June 11   David Payne family (4)
July 06   Jeff Thomas
July 14   Alex & Emily Lane
July 21   Earl Brown
Aug. 11   John McNicol
Aug. 31   Olivia Ellis
Sep. 14   Carolina Medina
Sep. 29   Matt Ellis
Oct. 26   Jessica Santana
Nov. 22   Ken Worsham

Total Losses: 42   **274 Families; 424 Members**

— 2015 —

The theme for this year was "With God We Can." The theme verse was Philippians 4:13.

Mission Sunday was on January 25. $122,618.76 was given. Several additional contributions came in later.

"Laborers Together With God" Sunday was on February 8. All members were given opportunities to serve in various capacities.

Our annual Sweetheart Banquet hosted by the Junior High Youth was on Saturday, February 21. This was for members fifty-five years or older and for members married twenty-five years or more.

Our Gospel Meeting was on March 1-4 with Phil Sanders speaking on "America's Only Hope."

Family Group meetings began in March with Groups 1-4 meeting in the homes of members on Tuesday nights.

Ladies Day' was on Thursday, April 17 with Celine Sparks of Huntsville, Alabama speaking on "Throwback Thursday: Old Time Religion."

Troy Spradlin gave a mission report on Sunday, April 19.

Evangelism Training for Youth was on May 1-2 with Lonnie Jones as the speaker.

Vacation Bible School was on June 21-24 with the theme "Building for God."

The Fifteenth Annual Leadership Training Camp for Young Men and Young Women was held on June 10-14 at the church building.

Josh Blackmer took a group of our teens on a mission trip to Whiteland, Indiana on June 26-July 3.

There was an Adult Mission Trip to Asuncion, Paraguay on July 6-14.

Jenkins Week at Central Florida Bible Camp was on July 19-25.

Upward Bound at Central Florida Bible Camp was on Saturday-Wednesday, July 25-29.

A Marriage Enrichment Seminar was held on September 11-13 with Neal Pollard as the speaker. The subject was "A Balanced Marriage."

Robert Martin gave a mission report on October 11.

Scott Shanahan gave a mission report on October 25.

Spiritual Enrichment Weekend at Central Florida Bible Camp was on Friday-Sunday, October 16-18. The theme was "Without Faith."

The Mount Dora Area-Wide Benefit Dinner was held at our building

— 2015 —

on Saturday, October 3.

The Twentieth Annual South Florida Lectureship, "Ready at His Coming," was held on Thursday-Sunday, November 5-8. Keynote speakers were Dan Jenkins, Melvin Otey, Stan Mitchell and B.J. Clarke. Breakout speakers were Stan Mitchell, Mark Blackwelder, B.J. Clarke, Melvin Otey, Bill Weaver, Kevin Patterson and Brenda Weaver.

Three of our elders and their wives were honored on Sunday, November 15 for their dedicated service for almost four decades: Johnny & Betty Davis; Joe & Marian Holland; and Jerry & Shirley Hopkins.

Elders
Johnny Davis
Dan Fuller
Joe Holland
Jerry Hopkins
Phil Porter

Evangelists
Dan Jenkins
David Sproule, II
Josh Blackmer

Deacons
Mike Archer
David Brown
Novel Brown
Chuck Clark
Victor Colage
Lance Collier
Jim Davis
Mike Erickson
Tim Fry
Jeff Goodale
Rick Hall
Bob Higbee
Gary Jenkins
Dick Kelley
Jeff Leslie
Paul Metzkes
Buzz Nelson
Jerry Pittman
Kevin Weeks

— 2015 —

Baptized (16)
Jan. 04 Amanda Fetting
Feb. 15 Pierre Irby
Mar. 04 Scott Lewis
Mar. 08 Nyla Hackshaw
May 14 Steven Livergood
May 23 Janice Osborne
May 24 Michael Paul Davidson
June 24 Mike Heitman
June 25 Haley Hall
July 19 Tracey Sue Brady
Sep. 06 Billy Ray Chancey
Sep. 10 Robin Landen
Sep. 22 Eddie Gooden
Oct. 04 Micah Trujillo
Dec. 07 Sandra Hanna
Dec. 12 Jenisa Kenty

Identified (22)
Jan. 04 Linda King
Mar. 08 Tracy Jamison
Apr. 12 Lauren Grimaldi
May 17 Morris McDaniel
May 31 Sharon Morrison
June 07 Deltom Lequernaqué
Aug 09 David, Jennifer, Tracy & Kaitlyn Jaress
Aug. 09 Shantal Martin
Aug. 09 Jacade & Susan Reynolds
Aug. 09 Peggy Delaney
Sep. 13 Jené A. Williams
Sep. 20 Brett & Hayden Lau
Oct. 04 Christina Kato
Oct. 25 Shaun, Emily & Simon Tyson
Dec. 13 Nahum Villard

Total Additions: 39

Restored (1)
May 17 Jeffrey Thomas

Weddings (1)
Oct. 10 Eldra Judge & Grace Hackshaw

Births (2)
Jan. 12 Sofia Annebelle McLeod
Oct. 20 Charlotte Madison Schuemann

— 2015 —

Died (5)
Jan. 27 Ross Stone
Mar. 06 Vera Day
Mar. 28 Jean McMasters
June 16 Gene Puckett
Aug. 01 Margaret Griffo

Moved Away (13)
Jan. 04 Warren Porter
Jan. 21 Brayden Gilles
Jan. 21 Jon & Priscilla Hoelzer
Jan. 21 Rodney Robinson
Mar. 08 Carolyn Preston
Apr. 01 Jennifer Anderson
Apr. 01 Andy Griffiths
June 10 Lenelle Crowell
June 10 Bethany Leslie
June 30 Helen Bashaw
Aug. 16 Pierre Irby
Aug. 16 Jeffrey Thomas
Sep. 01 Sabrina Lolo
Sep. 01 Lauren Grimaldi

Total Losses: 36   **284 Families; 446 Members**

— 2016 —

The theme for 2016 was "I'm Not Ashamed." The theme verse was Romans 1:16.

Mission Sunday was on January 31 and $154,084.34 was given.

Our Gospel Meeting was on March 6-9 with Sam Jones as the speaker. His subject was "You Can Be Just a Christian."

Our Thirty-Fourth Annual Ladies' Day was on Thursday, April 21 with Traci Sproule as the speaker. Her topic was "Daughters of the King."

Troy Spradlin gave a mission report on May 1.

Evangelism Training for Youth was on May 6-7 with Eric Lyons as the speaker. His topic was "Is the Bible Reliable?"

Grant Fuller worked as the summer intern.

Leadership Training Camp for Young Men and Young Women was on June 8-12.

Vacation Bible School was on June 19-22 with the subject "Knight's Quest: The Armor of God."

Our Ninety-Third Anniversary and Homecoming was on July 3. June Pack was honored for her long service to the congregation. She kept attendance for fifty-five years and served as church secretary since 1975.

Jenkins Week at Central Florida Bible Camp was on July 17-23.

Joey Treat made a mission report on September 11.

A Men's Fellowship was held on Saturday, September 24 with David Shannon as the speaker. His topic was "Strong Leaders for Strong Churches."

Spiritual Enrichment Weekend was on October 14-16 with the theme "I Can Do All Things."

Our Twenty-First Annual South Florida Lectureship was on November 3-6. The theme was "Wait On the Lord." Keynote speakers were Dan Jenkins, David Powell, Dave Miller and Paul Sain. Breakout speakers were Doug Burleson, Ben Griffin, Deb Miller, Gale Nelson and Daniel Stearsman.

The Hispanic congregation had been meeting in a rented place in Lake Worth, but when they lost that place, they began meeting in our church building again during this year, and we were glad to have them back.

— 2016 —

Elders
Johnny Davis
Dan Fuller
Joe Holland
Jerry Hopkins
Phil Porter

Evangelists
Dan Jenkins
David Sproule, II
Josh Blackmer

Deacons
Mike Archer
David Brown
Novel Brown
Chuck Clark
Victor Colage
Lance Collier
Jim Davis
Mike Erickson
Tim Fry
Jeff Goodale
Rick Hall
Bob Higbee
Gary Jenkins
Dick Kelley
Jeff Leslie
Paul Metzkes
Buzz Nelson
Jerry Pittman
Kevin Weeks

— 2016 —

Baptized (18)
Feb. 07 Bailey McDaniel
Apr. 03 Josiah Blackmer
Apr. 27 Karly Stone
May 01 Harrison Carter
May 01 Harrison Crotts
May 15 Daniel Lord
June 02 Andres & Angelica Fernandez
June 07 Cruz Fernandez
June 12 Carolyn Lord
July 15 Lydia Quinn
Aug. 14 Jason Halas
Sep. 20 Clarence Tipton
Oct. 02 Alice Nelson
Oct. 08 Aaron Ross
Oct. 08 Tonya Davis
Nov. 20 Aisha Femandez
Dec. 18 Rashana Green

Restored (3)
Jan. 31 Lynn Parker
Feb. 28 Tim Mahlbacher
Mar. 07 Cecilia Tipton

Births (2)
July 06 Blake Leslie
July 14 Katherine Grace Goodale

Identified (25)
Jan. 03 Robert Swayne
Feb. 22 Yolanda Stewart
Mar. 27 Carolina Medina
Apr. 10 Marvin & Maggie Dozier
Apr. 10 Alex Romigh
May 01 Henry & Bereather Williams
May 15 Lowell Flowers
May 15 Kathy Kelley
May 22 Karen Bibbee
May 22 Errol & Jessie Gower-Winter
June 05 Sharon Reitz
June 12 Michell Castonguay
July 10 Kirk & Mendy Crews
Aug. 28 Patricia Harrington
Sep. 11 Marie Yolette Achille
Sep. 11 Rose Jean-Baptiste
Oct. 23 Marcia Walker
Nov. 20 Lucy Bond
Nov. 20 Carolyn Preston
Nov. 20 Kyle & Sheena Sink

Total Additions: 46

— 2016 —

Died (6)
Mar. 24 Margaret Wade
Mar. 30 Kay Fish
May 12   Joe Quigley
July 27 Harold Armstrong
Aug. 12 Lowell Flowers
Oct. 12 Juanita Huser

Moved Away (22)
Jan. 22 Tracy Brady
Feb. 21 Tracy Jamison
May 04   Pearl El
May 07   Trevor & Tiffany Cheshier
June 24 Christina Kato
July 14 Adam Seal
July 14 Regina Mayne
Sep. 17 Kim Cullom
Sep. 17 Cecilia Tipton
Oct. 01 Shantel Martin
Oct. 25 Ben & Joycelyn Harriett
Oct. 26 Aryanna Duhl
Oct. 30 Linda King
Nov. 05 Clarence Tipton
Nov. 20 Monica Morando
Nov. 20 Peggy DeLaney
Dec. 14 David Jaress family (4)

Total Losses: 37   **291 Families; 457 Members**

— 2017 —

The theme for this year was "At His Cross." The theme verse was Galatians 2:20.

A series of Bible classes began in January at 5:00 p.m. Sunday evening in the Family Room taught by Dan Jenkins & David Sproule. The title was "Fortifying Your Faith." All members were encouraged to attend.

Mission Sunday was on January 29 and $151,622.85 was given.

The annual Sweetheart Banquet hosted by the Jr. High group was on Saturday, February 11.

Our Gospel Meeting this year was on March 5-8 with Dan Winkler as the speaker. The theme of the lessons was "The Embrace of God's Grace."

Our Thirty-Fifth Annual Ladies' Day was on Thursday, April 20 with Whitney Watson as the speaker. Her theme was "Ambassadors for Christ."

An Evangelism Training for Youth was on May 5-6 with J.D. Schwartz as the speaker.

Troy & Andrea Spradlin returned to the United States after serving for five years as missionaries in Paraguay and were honored by the congregation on Sunday, May 14.

The Seventeenth Annual Leadership Training Camp for Young Men and Young Women was on June 8-11 with thirteen young people attending.

Vacation Bible School was on June 18-21. This year's theme was "Under the Big Top."

A Senior High and Adult Mission Trip to Pilar, Paraguay was on June 26-July 4. Twelve attended.

Scott Shanahan gave a mission report on Sunday, July 2.

Jenkins Week at Central Florida Bible Camp was on July 23-29.

For five weeks, during part of July and August, all worship meetings were conducted in the Family Room while the main auditorium was being repaired and new carpet installed.

Richard Watson was ordained as an elder on Sunday, August 13.

Hurricane Irma paid us a visit on Sunday, September 10, so services were cancelled. No major damage was done to the church building, just vegetation cleanup.

Kirk Brothers was here for Super Sunday on October 1. The theme was "A Place to Come Home To."

— 2017 —

Robert Martin made his mission report on the Pacific Islands on October 8.

Spiritual Enrichment Weekend at Central Florida Bible Camp was on October 13-15.

Our Twenty-Second Annual South Florida Lectureship was on November 9-12. The theme was "Revive Us Again." Keynote speakers were Dan Jenkins, John Moore, David Lipe and Jay Lockhart. Breakout teachers were Bill Davis, Will Hanstein, James Mayo and Carla Moore.

Elders
Johnny Davis
Dan Fuller
Joe Holland
Jerry Hopkins
Phil Porter
Richard Watson

Evangelists
Dan Jenkins
David Sproule, II
Josh Blackmer

Deacons
Mike Archer
David Brown
Novel Brown
Chuck Clark
Victor Colage
Lance Collier
Jim Davis
Mike Erickson
Tim Fry
Jeff Goodale
Rick Hall
Bob Higbee
Gary Jenkins
Dick Kelley
Jeff Leslie
Paul Metzkes
Buzz Nelson
Jerry Pittman
Kevin Weeks

— 2017 —

Baptized (11)
Jan. 17 Tom Dolan
Mar. 26 Vivian Blackmer
Apr. 02 Adrienna Gadson
Apr. 10 Karen MacDonald
May 16 Ralph Williams
May 21 Sean Connor MacDonald
June 11 Katelyn Goodale
June 29 Jonathan Swayne
July 12 Sue Maisano
Aug. 11 Max Fonrose
Aug. 15 Cindy Beard

Identified (12)
Jan. 01 John Loftis
Jan. 18 Andy & Letha Anderson
Feb. 05 Carol Graff
Feb. 05 Jeannie Hamilton
Apr. 26 Heath Johnson
Apr. 30 Greg Bland
July 16 Judy Beard
Aug. 27 Jim Beard
Nov. 05 Julie Fontaine
Dec. 17 Michael & Quinia Morning

Restored (4)
July 16 Terri Hahn
Aug. 27 Sharon Banks
Dec. 10 Cornelius Brown
Dec. 24 Jennifer Anderson

Weddings (4)
Apr. 15 Aaron Ross & Tonya Davis
Apr. 21 David Bound, III & Casey Byerly
July 08 Jimmie Banks & Adrienne Gadson
Oct. 16 Michael Staley & Turkessa Fernander

Births (4)
Jan. 20 Lucas William Villard
Apr. 07 Merritt Landon Reeves
Oct. 10 Levi Keith Nelson
Dec. 28 David William Bound, IV

Total Additions: 27

— 2017 —

Died (5)
Feb. 22   Tommy Pauldo
Apr. 03   Sherrick Thomas
May 14   Ruth Milton
June 18   Marie Watson
June 31   Betty McQuinn

Moved Away (10)
Jan. 23   Jonathan Jordan
May 26   Shea Brown (TN)
July 23   Lauren Fuller (TN)
Aug. 13   Kelly Hall (TX)
Sep. 01   Kristen Fuller (TX)
Sep. 30   Sharon Morrison (TX)
Oct. 03   Linda Wolfe (MD)
Oct. 07   Lawrence D. Richardson (TX)
Dec. 17   Lynn & Cynthia Parker (Philadelphia)

Moved Membership (9)
July 16   Mary, Brandon & Chris Thomas (Stuart)
July 23   Jeff & Sharon Feeney (Jup.)
Sep. 24   Jaqua' Lewis (Suncoast)
Nov. 05   Paul & Kim Hensel (Jupiter/Tequesta)
Dec. 03   Alex Romigh (Stuart)

Total Losses: 27   **295 Families; 455 Members**

— 2018 —

The theme for this year was "28 Days." The theme verse was Romans 12:1-2.

Mission Sunday was on January 28, and $165,368.50 was given.

The annual Sweetheart Banquet hosted by the Junior High youth was on February 10.

Our Gospel Meeting this year was on March 11-14 with Glenn Colley as the speaker. The theme of the lessons was "Simply Amazing."

Our Thirty-Sixth Annual Ladies' Day was on Thursday, April 12 with Wendy Wadley as the speaker. Her theme was "Wise Women, Wise Words."

Our first "Power Up! A Recharge for Christian Men" was hosted on Saturday, May 5. About 100 men from area congregations came and heard five local preachers deliver fifteen-minute power lessons. The speakers were Terry Frizzell (Stuart), Ben Griffin (Suncoast), Bill Weaver (Gate Way), Daniel Stearsman (Okeechobee) and Gale Nelson (Miami-Gardens).

The theme for "Kick Start Your Summer" lessons was "Bind Us Together." Speakers were Terry Casey (May 23); Ron Brackett (May 30); Stan Bronson (June 6); Corey Glover (June 13); and Kevin Patterson (June 27).

Vacation Bible School was on June 17-20. The theme was "Discovering Bible Lands."

The Eighteenth Annual Leadership Training Camp for Young Men and Young Women was on June 29-July 1, with those attending giving lessons on Sunday morning, July 1. There were sixteen in attendance.

Kevin Weeks resigned as a deacon on July 15.

Jenkins Week at Central Florida Bible Camp was on July 22-28.

There was a Senior High and Adult Mission trip to Asuncion, Paraguay on July 3-11. Thirteen attended.

A South Florida Youth Summit was held on Saturday, August 4 with Joe Wells as the speaker. The theme was "Charged by Christ."

Wayne Parker gave a mission report on Sunday, September 9 and Joey Treat on Sunday, September 16.

Spiritual Enrichment Weekend was on October 12-14 at Central Florida Bible Camp.

Our Twenty-Third Annual South Florida Lectureship was on November 1-4. The theme was "Timely Answers to Ancient Questions." Speakers were Dan Jenkins, Tommy & Kathy Haynes, Ralph Gilmore, B.J. Clarke and Hiram Kemp.

— 2018 —

Elders
Johnny Davis
Dan Fuller
Joe Holland
Jerry Hopkins
Phil Porter
Richard Watson

Evangelists
Dan Jenkins
David Sproule
Josh Blackmer

Deacons
Mike Archer
David Brown
Novel Brown
Chuck Clark
Victor Colage
Lance Collier
Jim Davis
Mike Erickson
Tim Fry
Jeff Goodale
Rick Hall
Bob Higbee
Gary Jenkins
Dick Kelley
Jeff Leslie
Paul Metzkes
Buzz Nelson
Jerry Pittman

— 2018 —

Baptized (14)
Mar. 11 Ashley (Piper) Gerber
Mar. 29 Casey Commander
Apr. 01 Devin Eutsey
Apr. 22 Martin Barr
May 06 James Green
May 20 John Patrick
May 29 David Bound, III
June 10 Alexis Smith
Aug. 05 Sasha Smith
Sep. 05 Myke Civil
Oct. 07 Taylor Sue Price
Oct. 08 Joel & Jessica Ramirez
Oct. 28 Cody Price

Identified (10)
Jan. 18 Wiley Price
Feb. 04 Robert & Norma Mariano
Feb. 25 Patricia Patterson
Mar. 25 Sabrina Clayton
June 10 Glenn Gerber
July 01 Edwiygh Franck
Aug. 22 Martie Veverka
Sep. 09 Chad & Gorgeous Morgan

Restored (2)
Oct. 10 Anthony Reed
Dec. 30 Natalie Villa

Weddings (2)
June 09 Casey Commander & Aisha Fernandez
Oct. 19 Darin Summerlot & Katie Wagner

Births (1)
Jan. 17 Sebastian Charles Schuemann

Total Additions: 26

— 2018 —

Died (4)
Mar. 06 Helen Gardner
July 08 Shelton Howell
Sep. 25 Norman Smedley
Dec. 31 Nelson Watts

Moved Away (10)
Jan. 05 Jim & Cindy Beard
Jan. 07 Cassie Lavender (Orlando)
Jan. 14 Brett & Hayden Lau (Orlando)
July 12 Chad Brown (Tupelo, MS)
Aug. 19 Amanda Fetting (TN)
Sep. 10 Marcia Walker (VA)
Sep. 20 Judy Beard (Gainesville)
Oct. 10 Jason Halas

Moved Membership (8)
May 09   Mike & Julie Trujillo (Haverhill)
June 10 Clayton & Micah Trujillo (Haverhill)
July 15 Kyle & Sheena Sink (Stuart)
Aug. 05 Robin Landen (Jog Road)

Total Losses: 26   **295 Families; 455 Members**

— 2019 —

The annual theme was "Press On." The theme verse was Philippians 3:13-14.

On Sunday, January 6, eight new deacons were appointed: Kirk Crews, Cam Crotts, Bill Ingram, Jr., Nate Nelson, Lawrence Richardson, Shaun Tyson, Ivan Villard, Jr. and Kevin Weeks.

Our Fifteenth Mission Sunday was on January 20. The total amount given was $160,719.57.

The Sweetheart Banquet hosted by the Jr. High Youth was on Saturday, February 16.

The Gospel Meeting was on Sunday-Wednesday, March 3-6 with David Lipe from Baxter, Tennessee as the speaker. The main theme was "The Truth Shall Set You Free" and the lunchtime lesson theme was "Walking with Jesus."

The elders prayed with the congregation on Sundays at 5:30 p.m. during the month of March.

Josh, Cara & Vivian Blackmer went on a mission trip to Easter Island on March 13-24.

The Sr. High Spring Formal was on Saturday, April 13 at the Silver Ball Museum.

On Sunday, April 14, Joe Holland resigned from his position as an elder due to his declining health. A video of Joe was shown to the congregation along with a presentation made by the elders. Joe served from November 14, 1976 until April 14, 2019.

Our Thirty-Seventh Annual Ladies' Day was on Thursday, April 18. Becky Blackmon spoke on the topic of "Help Me Find the Time."

Our Second Annual Power Up! A Recharge for Christian Men was on Saturday, May 4. The theme was "The Anatomy of a Christian Soldier." The speakers were Josh Blackmer (Palm Beach Lakes), Corey Glover (Hallandale), Heath Johnson (Jog Road), Gale Nelson (Miami Gardens) and Kevin Patterson (Sebring).

On Sunday, May 19, PBL members honored David & Traci Sproule for twenty-five years of service at Palm Beach Lakes. They have been working with PBL since May 1994.

Promotion Sunday and the High School Graduates' Luncheon was held on Sunday, June 2. This year's graduates were Devin Eutsey, Max Fonrose, Kameron Heitler and Carolyn Lord.

The theme for our "Kick Start Your Summer" Series was "Aliens in a

— 2019 —

Strange Land." Speakers were Mike Baker (Concord Street), Ben Griffin (Suncoast), Aaron Johnson (West Broward) and Kevin Patterson (Sebring).

Vacation Bible School was on Sunday-Wednesday, June 16-19. The theme was "Rise & Shine for Jesus."

The Nineteenth Annual Leadership Training Camp for Young Men & Women was Wednesday-Sunday, June 26-30. The emphasis this year was, "What Does the Bible Say About Baptism?" There were eleven youth attendees.

The Senior High & Adult Mission Team went to Paraguay from July 3-10.

Jim Davis resigned as a deacon on July 21, so that he and Robin could focus their time on taking care of their parents.

Jenkins/Blackmer Week at Central Florida Bible Camp was Sunday-Saturday, July 21-27. There were over 140 campers this year.

The South Florida Youth Summit "Charged By Christ" was on Saturday, August 3. Andrew Weaver was the keynote speaker along with Jared Gaines (Stuart) and Chris Radcliffe (West Broward). This year's emphasis was "Charged By Christ to Lead the Charge."

Jeff Leslie led a mission team to the Bahamas on August 16-22. They worked with Tavaro Hanna in Eight Mile Rock and held a three-day Gospel Meeting.

On Wednesday, September 4, Palm Beach Lakes started planning for gathering funds to help brethren in four congregations in the northern Bahamas that were devastated by Hurricane Dorian. Supplies were bought the following weekend (roughly $30,000 worth), loaded on trucks on Sunday morning by PBL members and the first shipment was delivered to the shipping company in Ft. Lauderdale on Monday, September 9.

Josh Blackmer and Dan McLeod went on a mission trip to Easter Island on September 5-15.

A group of teens and chaperones led by Josh Blackmer went to RUSH Weekend at Freed-Hardeman University on September 26-29.

The elders prayed with the congregation on Sundays at 5:30 p.m. during the month of October.

Spiritual Enrichment Weekend, scheduled for October 11-13, was cancelled, so we could focus our attention on the Bahamas Hurricane Relief Efforts.

The annual Trunk-or-Treat hosted by the Jr. High Youth was on Satur-

— 2019 —

day, October 19.

PBL members were given the opportunity to write cards of encouragement on Sundays at 5:30 p.m. during the month of November. The meetings were led by one of our deacons, Lawrence Richardson.

Our Twenty-Fourth Annual South Florida Lectureship was on Thursday-Sunday, November 7-10. This year's theme was "Conformed to His Image." Speakers included Dominic Dos Santos (San Fernando, Trinidad); Sam Jones (Jackson, TN); Brent Kercheville (West Palm Beach, FL); Keith Mosher (Memphis, TN); Sheri Patterson (Sebring, FL); Justin Rogers (Henderson, TN); and Allen Webster (Jacksonville, AL).

Dominic Dos Santos presented the evening sermon following the lectureship.

To assist with the hurricane relief in the Bahamas, our first Work Team went to Freeport on November 11-18.

The Congregational Bonfire & Singing hosted by the Young Adults was on Saturday, November 16.

Robert Martin gave a mission report on Sunday, November 17 about his work in the Pacific Islands, as well as preached the morning sermon.

Ellison Delva, the preacher from Freeport, expressed thanks for the work being done in the Bahamas on Sunday, November 17, during morning services.

The Ladies' Soup Supper hosted by Traci Sproule was on Thursday, December 5.

The New Year's Eve Gathering was on Tuesday, December 31.

— 2019 —

Elders
Johnny Davis
Dan Fuller
Jerry Hopkins
Phil Porter
Richard Watson

Evangelists
Dan Jenkins
David Sproule
Josh Blackmer

Deacons
Mike Archer
David Brown
Novel Brown
Chuck Clark
Victor Colage
Lance Collier
Kirk Crews
Cam Crotts
Mike Erickson
Tim Fry
Jeff Goodale
Rick Hall
Bob Higbee
Bill Ingram, Jr.
Gary Jenkins
Dick Kelley
Jeff Leslie
Paul Metzkes
Buzz Nelson
Nate Nelson
Jerry Pittman
Lawrence Richardson
Shaun Tyson
Ivan Villard, Jr.
Kevin Weeks

— 2019 —

Baptized (6)
Apr. 28 Dana Daniel
July 18 Sabrina Swayne
         (TN, Mid South Youth Camp)
July 21 Nicholas & Stephanie Elridge
Aug. 14 Tamara Jean-Baptiste
Sep. 16 Alex Contreras
Oct. 03 Travis & Taylor Johnson
Oct. 06 Trey Higbee

Identified (6)
Mar. 17 Dion, Misty, Taylor, Kinsey &
         Graysen Hayes
Sep. 22 Roselette Charles

Other (2)
July 10 Lena Gadson
July 28 Rodney Woods

Weddings (3)
Jan. 11 Tom Masciarelli & Sharon
         Reitz
June 06 Michael Menendez & Astrid
         Arevalo
June 20 Caleb Boggs & Bethany
         Bertram

Births (3)
Jan. 15 Araminta Walker
Oct. 04 Darcy Eleanor Johnson
Dec. 10 Nautica Marie Thompson

Total Additions: 14

— 2019 —

Died (7)
Feb. 05 Silas Moses
Feb. 15 JoAnn Rogers
Apr. 08 Cora Lee Dennis
Apr.   Godfrey Pratt (Georgia)
May 08   Charles Fifield
Oct. 15 Janet Hickerson
Nov. 27 Charles Norton

Moved Away (14)
Feb. 17 Greg Bland (Texas)
Apr. 07 Danielle Carter (Georgia)
May 05   Esther Saintil
         (North Carolina)
June 23 Bethany Bertram (Missouri)
June 23 Glenn & Ashley Gerber
         (Las Vegas)
July 31 Henry & Josephine Bass
         (Gainesville)
Sep. 23 Astrid Menendez (California)
Nov. 10 Nicholas & Stephanie Elridge
         (Daytona Beach)
Nov. 13 Julio Aristy, III
         (Military Service)
Nov. 24 Sadie Tennant
         (Winter Garden)
Dec.   Carol Hardman (Vero Beach)

Moved Membership (4)
Jan. 27 Wiley Price (Third Street)
Feb. 24 Martie Veverka (Stuart)
May 19   Rick & Sherrie Tibbetts
         (Jupiter/Tequesta)

Total Losses: 32   **285 Families; 437 Members**

— 2020 —

The annual theme was "2020 Vision: Seeing What God Sees." The theme verse was Luke 10:23.

Our Sixteenth Mission Sunday was on January 26. The total amount given was $160,707.57.

The Sweetheart Banquet hosted by the Jr. High Youth was on Saturday, February 15.

The Gospel Meeting was on Sunday-Wednesday, March 1-4 with Eric Owens from Atlanta, Georgia as the speaker. The main theme was "Making My Salvation Sure" and the lunchtime lesson theme was "Getting to Know God."

On Wednesday, March 18, the Midweek Services were moved online due to the coronavirus.

The elders made their first weekly video to the congregation on March 20.

Sunday Worship Services on March 22 were held outside the building in six small groups (the congregation was divided alphabetically). Dan Jenkins preached the sermon, David Sproule led singing and Josh Blackmer presided during the Lord's Supper and Communion.

All Sunday Worship Services were moved online on March 29. Children's Bible classes were taught via Zoom Meetings. Adult classes and worship services were streamed as usual.

On Sunday, April 12, David Sproule started teaching a Bible class on "Sticking Together When We Can't Be Together."

Our Thirty-Eighth Annual Ladies' Day scheduled for Thursday, April 16 was cancelled. Brittany Owens-Davis was scheduled to speak on "Beauty for Ashes."

Family Group Meetings were held via Zoom on April 16 (Groups 1 & 2) and April 23 (Groups 2 & 3) and were led by Josh Blackmer and David Sproule.

The Sr. High Spring Formal scheduled for Saturday, April 18 was postponed.

Our Third Annual Power Up! A Recharge for Christian Men for Saturday, May 2 was rescheduled to May 1, 2021. The theme would have been "Empowered by God."

On Sunday, May 17, we were able to meet at the building again in four smaller groups (divided alphabetically).

On Sunday, May 24, we met at the building in three groups.

— 2020 —

On Sunday, May 31, we met at the building in two groups, still no evening worship. We started having Wednesday Bible Classes at the building again on June 3.

The theme for our "Kick Start Your Summer" Series was "It Is Well with My Soul." Speakers were Terry Frizzell (Stuart), Heath Johnson (Jog Road), and Mauricio Yegros (Coral Springs).

The Senior High & Adult Mission Team went to Dunnellon, Florida on Friday, June 12 until Wednesday, June 17 in lieu of the cancelled trip to Paraguay.

A one-day Vacation Bible School was held on Saturday, June 20 from 10:00 a.m. until 2:00 p.m. with a pizza lunch served. The theme was "God's Creation."

On Sunday, June 28, we were able to start meeting at the building for two divided morning worship services, Bible class (between the morning services) and evening worship. We continued having Wednesday Bible class at the building.

Promotion Sunday and the High School Graduates' Luncheon was held on Sunday, June 28. This year's graduates were Nyla Hackshaw and Kelly Sproule.

On Sunday, June 28, we began our Soldiers of Christ lessons again.

The Twentieth Annual Leadership Training Camp for Young Men & Women was on Wednesday-Sunday, July 1-4. The emphasis this year was, "Romans 12." There were 10 youth attendees.

On Wednesday, July 8, we went back to our normal devotional, Family Prayer and then Bible class format.

On Wednesday, July 15, "Stepping into the Bible" classes resumed.

Jenkins/Blackmer Week and Upward Bound at Central Florida Bible Camp were cancelled. Josh Blackmer planned a smaller Sunday-Wednesday retreat for the teens at Central Florida Bible Camp on July 12-15.

Dick Kelley resigned as deacon in July.

The Sr. High Spring Formal was rescheduled as a Masquerade Ball on Saturday, July 18. It was hosted by Dion & Misty Hayes.

The South Florida Youth Summit "Charged By Christ" was on Saturday, August 8. Chance Blackmer was the keynote speaker. This year's emphasis was "Charged By Christ to Fight the Good Fight."

Paul Metzkes was ordained as an elder on Sunday, August 16.

— 2020 —

The Creation Seminar with Jeff Miller was postponed until 2021.

Wayne Parker presented his mission report on Pohnpei on Sunday, September 13.

On Sunday, September 20, we returned to our regular worship schedule.

The annual Trunk-or-Treat hosted by the Jr. High Youth was on Saturday, October 17.

Our Twenty-Fifth Annual South Florida Lectureship was cancelled.

The Congregational Bonfire & Singing hosted by the Young Adults was on Saturday, November 14.

The Ladies' Soup Supper hosted by Traci Sproule was on Thursday, December 3.

Three of our deacons moved away: Lawrence Richardson moved to Texas in October; Shaun Tyson moved to Tennessee on December 22; and Kevin Weeks moved to Georgia the week of December 27.

The New Year's Eve Gathering was on Thursday, December 31.

— 2020 —

Elders
Johnny Davis
Dan Fuller
Jerry Hopkins
Paul Metzkes
Phil Porter
Richard Watson

Evangelists
Dan Jenkins
David Sproule
Josh Blackmer

Deacons
Mike Archer
David Brown
Novel Brown
Chuck Clark
Victor Colage
Lance Collier
Kirk Crews
Cam Crotts
Mike Erickson
Tim Fry
Jeff Goodale
Rick Hall
Bob Higbee
Bill Ingram, Jr.
Gary Jenkins
Jeff Leslie
Buzz Nelson
Nate Nelson
Jerry Pittman
Ivan Villard
Kevin Weeks

— 2020 —

Baptized (15)
Feb. 12 Melanie Weeks
Feb. 16 Ashley Alfaro
Feb. 23 Troy Alberga
Feb. 25 Gabrial Cutrer
Apr. 04 Marisa Reeves
Apr. 07 Keyana Gardner
Apr. 13 Enid Youngman
June 07 Jean Pieros
June 22 Trinity Franck
June 28 Idara Ikon
July 12 Janet Macdonald
Aug. 02 Connor Goodale
Oct. 13 Danielle Thunderhawk
Nov. 16 Kameron Heitler
Dec. 08 Sully Tyson

Births (4)
Feb. 12 Maddisun Jayne-Owen Dugger
Mar. 10 Abigail Rose Leslie
Aug. 09 Leticia Alfaro
Dec. 04 Jana Kerry-Ann Flores

Identified (3)
Feb. 02 John Judd
Mar. 08 Rick & Sherrie Tibbetts
Nov. 22 Sloan Davis

Restored (1)
June 17 Ricky Smith

Weddings (3)
Jan.   Riadh & Julie Fontaine-Fessi
Feb. 14 Jaime Flores & Natasha Campbell
Dec. 12 Robert Lupo & Reanna Johnson

Total Additions: 19

— 2020 —

Died (10)
Feb. 07 Sandra Daniels
May 07 Marie Thorpe
May 21 Hattie Daniels
Aug. 01 Karen Bibbee
Aug. 01 Harriet Morris
Aug. 11 Katie Summerlot
Sep. 29 Tom Martens
Oct. 18 Deidra Miley
Nov. 04 Linda Studer
Nov. 20 Sallie Moses

Moved Membership (3)
Feb. 12 Morris, Bailey & Bryce McDaniel

Moved Away (21)
Jun. Julie Fontaine-Fessi (Switzerland)
June 17 David Bound, III (Ohio)
June 20 Travis, Taylor & Darcy Johnson (Lake Mary, FL)
July Kaitlyn Donahue (Portland, OR)
Sep. Austin Reeves (Port St. Lucie)
Sep. Michell Castonguay (Fort Myers)
Sep. 29 Chris, Brittany & Nautica Thompson (TN)
Oct. Lawrence & Kay Richardson (TX)
Nov. 20 Chuck, Mary & Kari Reeves (Jackson, TN)
Dec. 22 Shaun, Emily, Simon & Sully Tyson (TN)
Dec. 27 Kevin, Stephanie & Melanie Weeks (GA)

Total Losses: 37   **278 Families; 419 Members**

— 2021 —

The annual theme was "Stronger Than Ever." The theme verse was Ephesians 6:10.

Nate Nelson resigned as deacon on January 10.

Our seventeenth Mission Sunday was on January 31. The total amount given was $190,240.73.

As part of Mission Sunday, the congregation was introduced to a new mission effort that Dan Jenkins and Josh Blackmer will be part of called "Palm Beach Lakes World Missions." They will be going out and helping other congregations locally, domestically and internationally.

The Youth & Young Adult Family Camping Trip was on February 5-8 at Highlands Hammock State Park.

The Sweetheart Banquet hosted by the Jr. High Youth was cancelled.

The Gospel Meeting with Dan Winkler was postponed to the last week of March. Dan was unable to hold the meeting due to health issues. It was held on Sunday-Wednesday, March 28-31 with Neal Pollard from Bowling Green, Kentucky as the speaker. The main theme was "A Call for New Testament Christianity" and the lunchtime lesson theme was "Church Friendly."

Our Thirty-Eighth Annual Ladies' Day was on Thursday, April 15. Brenda Weaver spoke on "Seeing Christ Through Our Brokenness."

The Sr. High Spring Formal was on Friday, April 23 at the Jupiter Country Club. The theme was "A Night on the Red Carpet."

Our Third Annual Power Up! A Recharge for Christian Men was on Saturday, May 1. The theme was "Empowered by God." The speakers were Dave Miller (Apologetics Press), Kevin Patterson (Sebring Parkway), Terry Frizzell (Stuart), and Heath Johnson (Jog Road).

Dave Miller (Apologetics Press) presented two lessons on "Is There a God?" on Sunday, May 2.

Jeff Miller (Apologetics Press) conducted a Seminar on Friday-Sunday, May 21-23 on "Christians Can Be Confident About Creation."

Promotion Sunday and the High School Graduates' Luncheon was held on Sunday, May 30. This year's graduates were Josiah Blackmer, Haley Hall, Daniel Lord, Sasha Smith and Tyler Williams.

The theme for our "Kick Start Your Summer" Series was "Better Than I Deserve." Speakers were Heath Johnson (Jog Road), Terry Casey (West Broward), Terry Frizzell (Stuart) and Kevin Patterson (Sebring).

A two-day Vacation Bible School was held on Saturday, June 19

— 2021 —

(10:00 a.m. until noon) and Sunday, June 20 (6:30-8:30 p.m.). The theme was "The Flood."

The Twenty-First Annual Leadership Training Camp for Young Men & Women was Wednesday-Sunday, June 23-27. The emphasis this year was a study of "The Sermon on the Mount." There were ten youth attendees.

There was an Ice Cream Social Send-Off for Robert & Reanna Lupo on Sunday evening, June 27. They left on Monday, June 28 to move to Knoxville, Tennessee to attend the Southeast Institute of Biblical Studies for the next two years.

One of our deacons, Cam Crotts, moved to St. Augustine on June 27.

The Senior High & Adult Mission Team went to Sneedville, Tennessee on Thursday-Wednesday, July 1-7.

Jenkins/Blackmer Week at Central Florida Bible Camp was on July 18-24, followed by Upward Bound on July 24-28.

The South Florida Youth Summit "Charged by Christ" with Clint Davison was postponed until August 2022.

Chad Wagner presented his mission report about the work in Nigeria, specifically on Nnanna Aforji, on Sunday, August 29.

There was a Congregational Prayer Meeting on Wednesday, September 1.

Joey Treat presented his mission report about the work in the Pacific Islands on Sunday, September 5.

Ron & Don Williams conducted an eight-lesson Grief Workshop on Friday-Sunday, September 24-26.

The annual Trunk-or-Treat hosted by the Jr. High Youth was on Saturday, October 16.

One of our deacons, Chuck Clark, passed away on Saturday, October 30.

Our Twenty-Fifth Annual South Florida Lectureship was on Thursday-Sunday, November 4-7. The theme was "He Who Promised Is Faithful." Speakers included Rick Brumback (Henderson, TN); John Deberry (Memphis, TN); Jeff Jenkins (Lewisville, TX); Gale Nelson (Miami, FL); Andy Robison (Moundsville, WV); Marsha Robison (Moundsville, WV); and Billy Smith (Henderson, TN).

Bill Ingram, Jr. resigned as deacon on November 28.

— 2021 —

The Ladies' Soup Supper hosted by Traci Sproule was on Thursday, December 2.

Dan & Judie Jenkins hosted a Year-End Get Together on December 7 for anyone who has ever attended the Monday Night or Tuesday Morning Bible Classes.

Robert Lupo presented a special Bible class on Sunday, December 19.

The New Year's Eve Gathering was on Friday, December 31 at 5:00 p.m. Instead of singing in the New Year, we held a Mac-and-Cheese Cook-Off.

— 2021 —

Elders
Johnny Davis
Dan Fuller
Jerry Hopkins
Paul Metzkes
Phil Porter
Richard Watson

Evangelists
Dan Jenkins
David Sproule
Josh Blackmer

Deacons
Mike Archer
David Brown
Novel Brown
Victor Colage
Lance Collier
Kirk Crews
Mike Erickson
Tim Fry
Jeff Goodale
Rick Hall
Bob Higbee
Gary Jenkins
Jeff Leslie
Buzz Nelson
Jerry Pittman
Ivan Villard, Jr.

— 2021 —

Baptized (6)
Mar. 07 Silas Balfour
Mar. 11 Brandan Widner
Sep. 25 Jonathan Wall
Oct. 24 Layla Courts-Buonadonna
Nov. 08 Markell Crawford
Nov. 21 David Caudill

Identified (8)
Feb. 01 Julie Watson
         (Jonah, Jane & Joy)
Mar. 28 Marie Telfort
June 27 Morris McDaniel
July 25 Hunter & Kaitlin Hinton
Sep. 26 Linda Allen
Sep. 26 Sherri Richmond
Dec. 19 Donald Seay

Restored (3)
May 05   Johnny Davis, Jr.
June 16 Owen Miley
Dec. 12 Maxine McCoy

Weddings (1)
Jan. 08 Sam Ford & Katie Sproule

Births (3)
Oct. 20 Petronillo Alfaro
Dec. 09 Asa Jermaine Walker
Dec. 14 Lilly Beth Villard

Total Additions: 17

— 2021 —

Died (8)

Feb. 01   Don Matter
Mar. 12   DeAndre Harmon
May 23   Annie Faison
June 16   Patricia Ventress
July 23   Adrienne Banks
Aug. 27   Les Sawyer
Oct. 30   Chuck Clark
Nov. 06   Norma Pratt

Moved Away (5)

May 12   Janet Macdonald
            (Tallahassee)
May   Tyrone Toson
June 27   Cam, Hollie, Harrison &
            Carter Crotts (St. Augustine)

Moved Membership (5)

July   Michael & Quinia Morning
            (Port St. Lucie)
Oct.   Morris McDaniel
            (Ft. Pierce)
Dec.   Jon & Jenny Jordan
            (Jog Road)

Total Losses: 30   **271 Families; 406 Members**

— 2022 —

The annual theme was "Imitators of God" The theme verse was Ephesians 5:1.

On January 2, Dion Hayes, David Lord & Lawrence Williams were appointed as deacons.

On January 9, PBL honored Dan & Judie Jenkins for forty years of service at PBL.

Our eighteenth Mission Sunday was on January 30. The total amount given was $214,479.42.

The Youth & Young Adult Family Camping Trip was February 4-7 at DuPuis Campground.

The Sweetheart Banquet hosted by the Jr. & Sr. High Youth was on Saturday, February 12.

On March 3, Jerry Pittman resigned as a deacon.

The Gospel Meeting was held on Sunday-Wednesday, March 6-9 with Phil Sanders from Edmond, Oklahoma as the speaker. The main theme was "Hungering for Truth" and the lunchtime lesson theme was "Answering 'Why?'"

On March 16, Jerry Hopkins resigned as an elder. He served as an elder for nearly forty-five years (October 17, 1971-October 12, 1980; July 27, 1986-March 16, 2022). Jerry and Shirley moved away to Riverview, Florida.

Our Thirty-Ninth Annual Ladies' Day was on Thursday, April 21. Carol Dodd was scheduled to speak but could not attend due to health issues. She passed away on April 30. Judie Jenkins, Cara Blackmer & Traci Sproule presented Carol's topic on "Why Am I Here?"

Our Fourth Annual Power Up! A Recharge for Christian Men was on Saturday, April 30. The theme was "Fellows in His Fellowship." Speakers were Neal Pollard (Bowling Green, KY), Lawrence Gilmore (WPB), Cy Cox (Jupiter) and Gale Nelson (Miami-Gardens).

The Sr. High Spring Formal was on Saturday, April 30 at Grande Italiano Restaurant. The theme was "Your Tell-Tale Heart."

The Shepherds invited PBL members to pray together with them at 5:30 p.m. during the months of May, August & November.

A Friends & Family Day with Neal Pollard was held on Sunday, May 1. The theme was "Jesus Holds the Keys." Lessons were at 9:00 a.m., 10:00 a.m. and 12:45 p.m. with a catered lunch from Pollo Tropical.

Promotion Sunday and the High School Graduates' Luncheon was held on Sunday, May 22. This year's graduates were Vivian Blackmer, Layla

— 2022 —

Carter, Katie Goodale, Taylor Hayes, Evrol Smith and Jonathan Swayne.

Robert Lupo worked as the summer intern.

Ivan Villard began his work as the Operations Manager on Friday, June 3.

The theme for our "Kick Start Your Summer" Series was "Living the Abundant Life." Speakers were Kevin Patterson (Sebring), Terry Frizzell (Stuart), Terry Casey (West Broward), and Douglas Alvarenga (PBL).

Vacation Bible School was held on Sunday-Wednesday, June 5-8. The theme was "Fearless."

The Twenty-Second Annual Leadership Training Camp for Young Men & Women was on Wednesday-Sunday, 22-26. The emphasis this year was "The Story of the Bible." There were five youth attendees.

The Senior High & Adult Mission Team went to Parma, Idaho on July 5-12.

Jenkins/Blackmer Week at Central Florida Bible Camp was on July 17-23.

Jeff Leslie took a team to Marsh Harbour, Bahamas on August 12-15 to encourage the congregation and for the dedication of their new building after the previous one was heavily damaged in Hurricane Dorian.

The South Florida Youth Summit "Charged by Christ" with Clint Davison was on Saturday, August 13.

Tavaro Hanna presented a report on his work in Eight Mile Rock, Grand Bahama on Sunday, August 28.

David Sproule started teaching "His Kids" Class on Sundays at 5:30 p.m. for age 3 and up.

Wayne & Tami Roberts held a Marriage Seminar on Friday-Saturday, September 16-17. The theme was "His Shoes. Her Shoes."

There was a Benefit Dinner for Mount Dora Children's Home on Saturday, October 15.

"Coming Home" Sunday was on Sunday, October 16. PBL members wrote letters of encouragement to former members who still live in the area leading up to this Sunday.

The annual Trunk-or-Treat hosted by the Jr. & Sr. High Youth was on Saturday, October 22.

Our last House-to-House/Heart-to-Heart labeling night was on Sunday, October 30. It is now being mailed directly to homes in our area.

— 2022 —

Our Twenty-Sixth Annual South Florida Lectureship was on Thursday-Sunday, November 3-6. The theme was "Questions Surrounding the Second Coming." Speakers included Don Blackwell (Cookeville, TN); Doug Burleson (Henderson, TN); Jason Jackson (Jackson, TN); Denny Petrillo (Denver, CO); and Neal Pollard (Bowling Green, KY). There was no ladies' class this year.

The Ladies' Soup Supper hosted by Traci Sproule was on Thursday, December 1.

The New Year's Eve Gathering was discontinued this year.

— 2022 —

Elders
Johnny Davis
Dan Fuller
Paul Metzkes
Phil Porter
Richard Watson

Evangelists
Dan Jenkins
David Sproule
Josh Blackmer

Deacons
Mike Archer
David Brown
Novel Brown
Victor Colage
Lance Collier
Kirk Crews
Mike Erickson
Tim Fry
Jeff Goodale
Rick Hall
Dion Hayes
Bob Higbee
Gary Jenkins
Jeff Leslie
David Lord
Buzz Nelson
Lawrence Williams

— 2022 —

Baptized (17)
Jan. 28 Jettie Sweetenburg
Mar. 06 Susan Preston
Mar. 12 Ashley Blumhof
Mar. 21 Caila Buonadonna
Mar. 21 Todd Juckett
May 27 Islay Rodriguez
June 12 Karen Lester
June 22 Emma Reeves
June 27 Suzanne Weber
June 28 Jack Holoman
June 29 Evangelina Rivas
Aug. 12 Janice Cooley
Aug. 13 David Perez
Aug. 16 David Whipple
Nov. 07 Islay Rodriguez, Jr.
Nov. 27 Jamie Green
Dec. 11 Crystal Burroughs

Identified (14)
Mar. 06 Robin Landen
Mar. 06 Allison & Joseph Snyder
Apr. 03 Addison Collins
July 10 Tom Garrison
Aug. 14 Allan Zamora & Francis Morales (Emma & Mateo)
Aug. 14 Krystian Dubuisson
Aug. 14 Cris Cuevas
Sep. 18 Juna Dorcely
Sep. 17 Bethany Leslie
Oct. 23 Cristian & Lisa Suarez (Olivia & Nathan)
Dec. 18 Cecilia Tipton

Restored (2)
Mar. 27 Sadie Myrie
Nov. 20 Sylvester Jackson

Weddings (2)
Nov. 12 Todd Juckett & Caila Buonadonna
Nov. 07 David Perez & Natalie Villa

Births (2)
Feb. 07 Hattie Nell Hinton
Aug. 12 Ariyah Dubuisson

Total Additions: 33

— 2022 —

Died (10)
Feb. 01 Grace Shaw
Feb. 07 Joe Holland
Mar. 27 Connye Plouffe
Apr. 23 Willie Shaw
May 21 Johnny Mark Davis
June 16 Bill Ingram, Sr.
Oct. 15 Joyce Barnhouse
Oct. 17 Glen Dawson
Nov. 05 Richard & Judy Lerro

Moved Membership (6)
Jan. 06 Cornelius & Andrea Henderson (Deerfield Beach)
Sep. 04 Sue Shelt (Stuart)
Oct. 12 Sandy Mann (Jog Road)
Oct. 26 Gabby Newby (Delray)
Nov. 14 Betsy Donahue

Moved Away (22)
Feb. 07 Ken & Connie Tipton (TN)
Mar. 16 Jerry & Shirley Hopkins (Riverview, FL)
Apr. 14 Bonnie Arthur (Ocala, FL)
Apr. 15 Terry Denton Hatfield (Hernando, FL)
Apr. 17 Helen Burney (AL)
Apr. 23 Gabrial Cutrer (OK)
June 12 Meagan Metzkes (Tampa, FL)
June 20 Errol & Jessie Gower-Winter (Lake Placid, FL)
June 20 Robert Swayne (TN)
June 22 David Thorpe (Jacksonville, FL)
Aug. 22 Gary & Angie Seames (MO)
Aug. 28 Casey Commander (Yulee, FL)
Sep. 19 Kathy Kelley (North Florida)
Oct. 07 Carolyn Preston (GA)
Oct. 12 Louise Phillips (Okeechobee)
Nov. 27 Sam & Peggy Simpkins (VA)
Dec. 18 Andy & Letha Anderson (Winter Haven, FL)

Total Losses: 61 **256 Families; 377 Members**

— 2023 —

The annual theme was "A Chapter a Day." The goal this year was to read through the entire New Testament (five chapters each week with a Bible marking day and a Day of Reflection).

Our nineteenth Mission Sunday was on January 29. The total amount given was $259,125.20.

The Youth & Young Adult Family Camping Trip was January 20-22 at Fisheating Creek.

The Sweetheart Banquet hosted by the Jr. & Sr. High Youth was on Saturday, February 11.

Mike Archer resigned as deacon on February 19.

The Gospel Meeting was held on Sunday-Wednesday, March 5-8 with Jeff Jenkins from Lewisville, Texas as the speaker. The main theme was "God's Glorious Plan for Us" and the lunchtime lesson theme was "Snapshots from Revelation.'"

Our Fortieth Annual Ladies' Day was on Thursday, April 20. Lacy Crowell spoke on "Jesus, Our Loving Shepherd."

The Sr. High Spring Formal was on Saturday, April 29 at the Silverball Museum. The theme was "A Night with the Pinball Wizard."

Our Fifth Annual Power Up! A Recharge for Christian Men was on Saturday, May 6. The theme was "Disabling the Devil's Devices." Speakers were Steve Higginbotham (Knoxville, TN), Jonny Singh (Lake Placid), Terry Frizzell (Stuart) and Gale Nelson (Miami-Gardens).

Steve Higginbotham was the guest speaker for morning services on Sunday, May 7. The theme was "Home, Sweet Home."

Promotion Sunday was on Sunday, May 14.

Simon Tyson began his summer internship on Sunday, May 21 and will work until the end of July.

The High School Graduates' Luncheon was held on Sunday, May 28. This year's graduates were Marco Carmona, Kinsey Hayes, Alice Nelson, Cody Price and Karly Stone.

The theme for our Kick Start Your Summer Series was "Model Prayers in the Bible." Speakers were Terry Casey (West Broward), Gale Nelson (Miami-Gardens), Terry Frizzell (Stuart), and Kevin Patterson (Sebring).

It was announced on Sunday, May 28 that Josh and Cara Blackmer would begin a new evangelistic phase of "Answering Macedonian Calls" (formerly known as "Palm Beach Lakes World Missions"). Josh and Cara have sold their home and will be traveling around the United States in an RV,

— 2023 —

helping smaller congregations.

Jeff Leslie led a mission team to Eight Mile Rock, Bahamas on June 1-5 to go door-knocking to promote their gospel meeting. There were twelve members who joined him on the mission trip.

Robert Lupo began his work at PBL on Sunday, June 11.

Our Vacation Bible School was on Sunday-Wednesday, June 11-14. The theme was "Operation: Creation."

David Sproule held a one-day "His Kids" Camp for boys and girls age 5-11 at the church building on Friday, June 9.

PBL's 100th Anniversary (1923-2023) was celebrated on the weekend of July 1-2. Former members were invited to come back and enjoy a time of fellowship and memories.

Elders
Johnny Davis
Dan Fuller
Paul Metzkes
Phil Porter
Richard Watson

Evangelists
Dan Jenkins
David Sproule
Josh Blackmer
Robert Lupo

Deacons
David Brown
Novel Brown
Victor Colage
Lance Collier
Kirk Crews
Mike Erickson
Tim Fry
Jeff Goodale
Rick Hall
Dion Hayes
Bob Higbee
Gary Jenkins
Jeff Leslie
David Lord
Buzz Nelson
Lawrence Williams

— 2023 —

Baptized (4)
Jan. 22 Max Eizaga
Jan. 30 Casey Crews
Jan. 30 Claire Crews
Mar. 07 Amira Hill

Identified (1)
Mar. 12 Malita Robinson

Births (3)
Jan. 23 David Alexander Perez
Feb. 14 Isabel Karissa Flores
Feb. 27 Amelia Reese Leslie

Total Additions: 5

— 2023 —

Died (3)
Apr. 15   Cheryl Floyd
Apr. 19   Betty Sanders
May 10   Marian Holland

Moved Away (3)
Jan. 04   Teresa Williams (WI)
Mar. 13   Pat Harrington (MI)
Apr. 15   Jettie Sweetenburg (SC)

Moved Membership (1)
May 03   Steven Livergood (Stuart)

Total Losses: 8   **As of June 1: 261 Families; 378 Members**

— Mission Sunday —

Year	Amount
2004	$126,948.59
2005	$120,620.06
2006	$123,590.00
2007	$122,547.10
2008	$105,959.35
2009	$101,247.83
2010	$121,018.99
2011	$112,787.90
2012	$107,737.86
2013	$122,378.77

Year	Amount
2014	$120,367.12
2015	$126,496.04
2016	$156,283.00
2017	$150,629.50
2018	$201,348.50
2019	$213,339.00
2020	$161,884.57
2021	$190,240.73
2022	$219,284.42
2023	$268,210.20

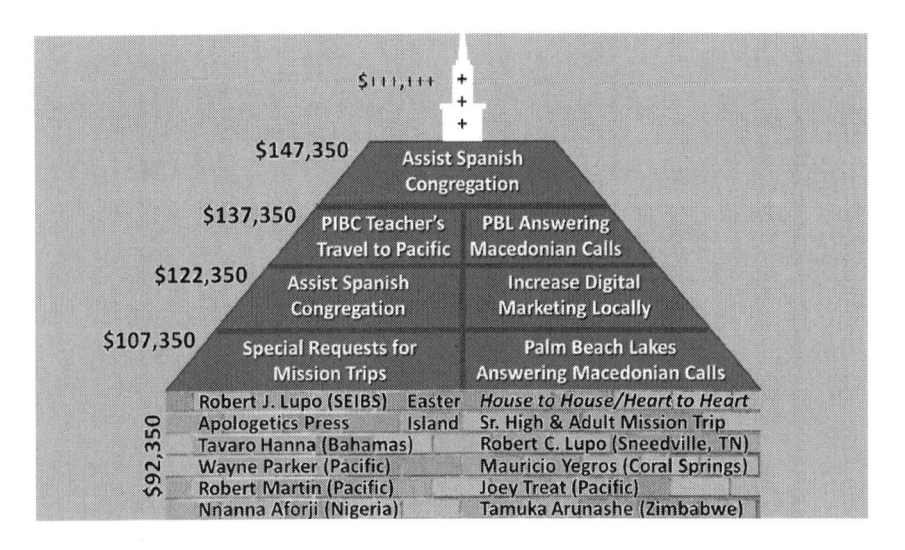

$111,111

$147,350 — Assist Spanish Congregation

$137,350 — PIBC Teacher's Travel to Pacific | PBL Answering Macedonian Calls

$122,350 — Assist Spanish Congregation | Increase Digital Marketing Locally

$107,350 — Special Requests for Mission Trips | Palm Beach Lakes Answering Macedonian Calls

$92,350 —
- Robert J. Lupo (SEIBS)
- Apologetics Press
- Tavaro Hanna (Bahamas)
- Wayne Parker (Pacific)
- Robert Martin (Pacific)
- Nnanna Aforji (Nigeria)
- Easter Island
- House to House/Heart to Heart
- Sr. High & Adult Mission Trip
- Robert C. Lupo (Sneedville, TN)
- Mauricio Yegros (Coral Springs)
- Joey Treat (Pacific)
- Tamuka Arunashe (Zimbabwe)

"And He said to them, "Go into all the world and preach the gospel to every creature. 16 He who believes and is baptized will be saved; but he who does not believe will be condemned."" (Mark 16:15)

*Totals listed are for the entire year (on Mission Sunday and during the rest of the year).

— Missionaries —

Year	Name	Location
1960s-1975	Jack Fogarty	Rio Piedras, Puerto Rico
1965-1968	Marcus Crews	Australia
1969-1973	Gerald Pace	Tasmania, Australia
1971-1974	Dane Waggoner	San Juan, Puerto Rico
	Franck Blenman	St. Michael, Barbados W.I.
1973-1975	George O'Briant	Kamloops, British Columbia
1973	Joe Salmon	Tasmania, Australia
1975	Charles Salmon	Tasmania, Australia
1974-1978	Ray Winn	Tasmania, Australia
1975	Earl Clevenger	San Juan, Puerto Rico
1977-1982	Buddy Lawrenson	Cape Town, South Africa
1979	Walter Ashenfelter	South Boston, VA
1979	Wade Bates	Astoria, OR
1979	Martin Davis	Clarksville, GA
1979	Tom Fairley	Tasmania, Australia
1979	Michael Lawler	Wallingford, CT
1986-1995	Bobbis Evdoxiades	Athens, Greece
1987-1995	Ronald Coleman	London
1987-2005	Ray Leonard	South Africa
1989-Present	Robert Martin	Pacific Islands
1991-1994	Francis York	Jamaica
1992-1994	Jon Macon	Madras, India
1992-1995	Michael Dykes	Guyana
1992-1996	Bill Nicks	Caribbean
1993-2002	Ronnie Crocker	Prison Work
1994-1998	Dumas Lafleur	Haitian work in Miami, FL

— Missionaries —

Year	Name	Location
1995-2005	Junot Joseph	Haitian work in Miami, FL
1994-Present	Nnanna Aforji	Nigeria, West Africa
1994-Present	Tamuka Arunashe	Zimbabwe, Africa
2002-2004	Surendra Singh	Trinidad
2004-Present	Joey Treat	Pacific Islands
2005-2011	Chris Fry	Paraguay
2006-2011	Jason Quashie	Marsh Harbour, Bahamas
2009-2014	Josh Blackmer	Paraguay & Easter Island
2012-2017	Scott Shanahan	Pacific Islands
2012-2017	Troy Spradlin	Paraguay
2013-Present	Mauricio Yegros	Coral Springs, Florida
2017-Present	Wayne Parker	Pohnpei, NW Pacific Islands
2018-Present	Tavaro Hanna	Eight Mile Rock, Bahamas
2019-Present	Robert C. Lupo	Sneedville, TN

— Mission Works —

Name	Location
"In Search of the Lord's Way" TV Program	Edmond, OK
Apologetics Press	Montgomery, AL
Christian Courier	Jackson, TN
House to House/Heart to Heart	East Ridge, TN
Pacific Islands Bible College	Pacific Islands
PBL Answering Macedonia Calls	Palm Beach Gardens, FL
Trinidad School of Preaching	San Fernando, Trinidad
Truth for Today World Mission School	Searcy, AR

These lists are incomplete. We apologize for omissions and inaccuracies.

— Preaching School Students —

Year	Name	Location
1977-1978	Wade Bates	Sunset School of Preaching
1968-1970	Dane Waggoner	Sunset School of Preaching
1982-1984	Steve Ellis	Memphis School of Preaching
1984-1985	Bruce DeMoss	Memphis School of Preaching
1984-1986	Jay Winter	Memphis School of Preaching
1990-1992	Kevin Joy	Florida School of Preaching
1991-1993	Ronnie Crocker	Memphis School of Preaching
1992-1994	Jonathan Jenkins	Memphis School of Preaching
1993-1995	Junot Joseph	Florida School of Preaching
1995-1996	Everett Chambers	Brown Trail School of Preaching
2002-2004	Al Washington	Southwest School of Bible Studies
2007-2009	Troy Spradlin	Southwest School of Bible Studies
2018-2019	Brad Shelt	Sunset School of Preaching
2021-2023	Robert J. Lupo	Southeast Institute of Biblical Studies

These lists are incomplete. We apologize for omissions and inaccuracies.

— Gospel Meetings —

Year		Speaker
1971	Fall	Cline Paden
1972	Spring	Wyatt Sawyer
1973	Fall	Johnny Ramsey
1974	Spring	Cleon Lyles
1974	Fall	Maxie Boren
1975	Spring	Paul Faulkner
1975	Spring	Otis Gatewood
1975	Fall	Jim Waldron
1976	Spring	Elmer Morgan
1976	Fall	Dan Jenkins
1977	Spring	Wyatt Sawyer
1978	Spring	Maxie Boren
1979	Spring	Bill Smith
1980	Spring	Avon Malone
1981	Spring	Jim Mankin
1981	Fall	Jack Exum
1982	Spring	Johnny Ramsey
1983	Spring	Maxie Boren
1984	Spring	Willard Collins

Year		Speaker
1985	Spring	Tom Holland
1986	Spring	Goebel Music
1987	Spring	Neal Pryor
1988	Spring	Maxie Boren
1989	Spring	Johnny Ramsey
1990	Spring	Tom Holland
1991	Spring	Bert Thompson
1992	Spring	Jerry Moffitt
1993	Spring	James Meadow
1994	Spring	Wendell Winkler
1995	Spring	Tom Holland
1996	Spring	Garland Elkins
1997	Spring	Richard Melson
1998	Spring	Hardeman Nichols
1999	Spring	Dave Miller
2000	Spring	Tom Holland
2001	Spring	Ralph Gilmore
2002	Spring	Richard Melson
2003	Spring	Glenn Colley

— Gospel Meetings —

Year	Theme	Speaker
2004	Restoring God's Plan	Dave Miller
2005	Looking Unto Jesus	David Lipe
2006	Seeking the Old Paths	Hardeman Nichols
2007	Discovering the Truth	Sam Jones
2008	Why You Should Be a Christian	Phil Sanders
2009	Back to Basics	Glenn Colley
2010	Power to Become	Tommy Haynes
2011	If This Was the Only Book I Ever Followed…	Sam Jones
2012	The Essentials	Neal Pollard
2013	The Freedom of Forgiveness	Dan Winkler
2014	Finally…Some Good News!	David Lipe
2015	America's Only Hope	Phil Sanders
2016	You Can Be Just a Christian	Sam Jones
2017	The Embrace of God's Grace	Dan Winkler
2018	Simply Amazing	Glenn Colley
2019	The Truth Shall Set You Free	David Lipe
2020	Making My Salvation Sure	Eric Owens
2021	A Call for New Testament Christianity	Neal Pollard
2022	Hungering for Truth	Phil Sanders
2023	God's Glorious Plan for Us	Jeff Jenkins

— Ladies' Days —

Year	Theme	Speaker
1983		PBL Ladies
1984		PBL Ladies
1985	The Christian Woman Today	Aileen Belden Evelyn Coleman Loni Brown June Haines Judie Jenkins Joy Judd
1986	How to Teach Children More Effectively	Kim Leslie Carol Dodd
1987	Far Above Rubies	Shirley Hopkins Pat Brown
1988	Love: The Golden Chain That Binds	Peggy Hatcher Tommie Cain
1989	The Blessings of Adversity	Mona Faulkner
1990	Take a Little Honey	Gerry Nicks
1991	Apples of Gold	Inell Ingram Judie Jenkins
1992	Because He Lives, I Can Face Tomorrow	Jane Foster
1993	Reaching for Rainbows	Debi Watson
1994	Back to Basics	Elsie Hufford
1995	Mirror, Mirror	Rose Coleman
1996	Lessons I Have Learned from Children	Betty Davis Shirley Hopkins Gwen Lyons
1997	The Beauty of Jesus	Carolyn McWhorter
1998	A New Beginning	Barbara Mackifield
1999	Tomorrow May Be Too Late	Jean Reel
2000	Lord, Teach Me to Pray	Jeanie Langford

— Ladies' Days —

Year	Theme	Speaker
2001	Because He Lives	Julie Jenkins
2002	Gifts of Hospitality	Laurel Sewell
2003	God's Woman	Rose Coleman
2004	Lifting Others As You Climb	Mattie Jackson
2005	The Bread of Life	Becky Blackmon
2006	M&M's	Becky Blackmon
2007	Remodeling Your House	Becky Blackmon
2008	The Treasure of Contentment	Melanie Jenkins
2009	Lord, Make Me a Barnabas	Becky Blackmon
2010	His Eye Is on the Sparrow	Roberta Edwards
2011	He Is Lord of Lords	Cindy Colley
2012	Striving to Win	Kathy Haynes
2013	Choosing to Serve	Becky Blackmon
2014	The Bride of Christ	Kathy Pollard
2015	Throwback Thursday: Old Time Religion	Celine Sparks
2016	Daughters of the King	Traci Sproule
2017	Ambassadors for Christ	Whitney Watson
2018	Wise Women, Wise Words	Wendy Wadley
2019	Help Me Find the Time	Becky Blackmon
2020	Cancelled Due to Covid	
2021	Seeing Christ Through Our Brokenness	Brenda Weaver
2022	Why Am I Here? (Carol Dodd's Lesson Presented By PBL Preacher's Wives)	Judie Jenkins Traci Sproule Cara Blackmer
2023	Jesus, Our Loving Shepherd	Lacy Crowell

— South Florida Lectureships —

Year	Theme
1996	Guided By the Light
1997	The Christian Home in a Secular Society
1998	Fundamentals of Our Faith
1999	Life & Godliness: Studies in 1 & 2 Peter
2000	Worship That Pleases God
2001	Here Am I, Send Me
2002	Applying Acts in the 21st Century
2003	Written for Our Admonition: Great Lessons from the Old Testament
2004	Stand in the Gap
2005	Respect for God's Word
2006	Pearls From Proverbs
2007	Increase My Faith
2008	The Joys of Christianity
2009	We Would See Jesus: The Son of God
2010	We Would See Jesus: The Son of Man
2011	Heaven's Home-Improvement Workshop
2012	I Love the Church of Christ Because...
2013	God Has Spoken!
2014	Part of the Family
2015	Ready At His Coming
2016	Wait on the Lord
2017	Revive Us Again
2018	Timely Answers to Ancient Questions
2019	Conformed to His Image
2020	Cancelled Due to Covid

— South Florida Lectureships —

Year	Theme
2021	He Who Promised Is Faithful
2022	Questions Surrounding the Second Coming
2023	You Can Trust the Bible

— Men Who Have Served As Elders —

Year	Name
1964-1968	Jean McMasters
1964-1979	Hayward Milton
1964-1981	Don Spurlock
1964-1970	Alvin Witt
1970-1986	Harold Keathley
1971-1980 1986-2022	Jerry Hopkins
1972-1975	Fred Faulkner
1975-1977	Jesse Ford
1976-2003 2007-Present	*Johnny Davis
1976-2019	Joe Holland
1980-1984	Bill Ingram, Sr.
1980-1984	Dewayne Lanham
1984-1996	Don Hickerson
1986-1988	Doug Carmack
1991-2007	Stan Bronson
2000-2005	Dan McLeod
2003-2011	Don Dodd
2005-2011	Greg Morris
2007-2008	Willie Smith

Year	Name
2011-Present	*Dan Fuller
2012-Present	*Phil Porter
2017-Present	*Richard Watson
2020-Present	*Paul Metzkes

"Shepherd the flock of God which is among you, serving as overseers, not by compulsion but willingly, not for dishonest gain but eagerly; nor as being lords over those entrusted to you, but being examples to the flock."

(1 Pet. 5:2-3)

*Currently Serving as an Elder

— Men Who Have Served As Deacons —

Year	Name
1965-1976, 2004-2007	Johnny Davis
1965-1976	Bob Haines
1965-1971	Jerry Hopkins
1965	Paul Jordan
1966-2006	Pete Brown
1966-1972	Lowell Flowers
1966-1980, 1990-2000	Bill Ingram, Sr.
1966-1971	Charles Kulp
1966-1981	Tom Mitchell
1966-1997	Bill Powell
1966-1977	Doug Renahan
1970-1973	Marty Wingo
1973-1984	Gerald Bobo
1973-1975, 1979-1984	Jesse Ford
1973-1980	Dewayne Lanham
1973-1976	Gary Morton
1973-2002	Russell Waggoner
1975-1986	Doug Carmack
1975-1982	Tom Holaday
1979-1983	Hugh Horrocks
1979-2001	Carl Mack
1979-1981	Austen Moore
1982-1995	David Fenn
1982-1983	Jack Kline

Year	Name
1982-2000	David Sproule
1982-2009	Scott Studer
1983-2003	Don Dodd
1983-1984	Don Hickerson
1983-1984	Dewight Lanham
1983-1992	Joe Alcock
1984-Present	*Jeff Leslie
1984-1987	Red Springer
1984-1994	Jim Whitesides
1985-1990	Dave Holaday
1985-1998	Jim Howell
1985-2000	Dan McLeod
1985-2002	Jerry Pittman
1985-1990	Jim Rogers
1986-2007, 2012-Present	*Mike Erickson
1988	Bob Medlock
1988-2005	Greg Morris
1988-1990	Ron Brackett
1988-1991	Stan Bronson
1988-1999	Joe Maloney
1988-1993	Chuck Milton
1990-1991	Tom Brown
1990-2003	Ron Cullom
1990-1996	John Hoelzer

— Men Who Have Served As Deacons —

Year	Name
1990-1998 / 2004-2012 / 2019-2021	Bill Ingram, Jr.
1990-1993	Kevin Keathley
1990-2006	Dirk Summerlot
1991-1994	Mike Barrios
1993-1996	Jeff Feeney
1993-2011	Dan Fuller
1993-2006	Harold Pack
1994-Present	*David Brown
1994-2000	Ephriam Davis
1994-2012	Phil Porter
1996-2000	Bill Boyd
1996-2004 / 2009-Present	*Gary Jenkins
2000-Present	*Novel Brown
2000-Present	*Rick Hall
2000-2002	John Mayne
2000-Present	*Buzz Nelson
2003-Present	*Tim Fry
2003	Brian Jones
2003-2007	Willie Smith
2003-2011	Richard Watson
2004-2007	Aaron Bronson
2004-Present	*Jeff Goodale
2004-2014	Paul Hensel
2004-2006	Freddy Shelley

Year	Name
2006-2009	Richard Ahlijah
2006-2021	Chuck Clark
2006-Present	*Lance Collier
2006-2009	Mike Ellis
2006-2020	Richard Kelley
2006	Cleave Pamphile
2006-2008	David Thorpe
2006-2007	Pete Zubriski
2009-2010	Kane Campbell
2009-Present	*Victor Colage
2012-2023	Mike Archer
2012-2013 / 2019-Present	*Kirk Crews
2012-2019	Jim Davis
2012-Present	*Bob Higbee
2012-Present	Paul Metzkes
2012-2018 / 2019-2020	Kevin Weeks
2019-2021	Cam Crotts
2019-2021	Nate Nelson
2019-2021	Lawrence Richardson
2019-2020	Shaun Tyson
2019-2022	Ivan Villard, Jr.
2022-Present	*Dion Hayes
2022-Present	*David Lord
2022-Present	*Lawrence Williams

*Currently Serving as a Deacon

— Men Who Have Served As Preachers —

Year	Name	Location
1925-1928	Henry Clay Geer	Conniston Road
1928-1931	Warren Colson	Conniston Road
1931-1932	Alfred Traylor	Conniston Road
1932-1935	Ethany Shoulders	Conniston Road
1935-1939 1942-1945	Russell King	Conniston Road
1939-1942	M. Cecil Perryman	Conniston Road
1945-1948	Bill Floyd	Conniston Road
1948-1950	Iverson L. Boles	Conniston Road North Olive Avenue
1950-1954	John Renshaw	North Olive Avenue
1955-1959	Hugh Piper	North Olive Avenue
1959	Eugene Pitts	North Olive Avenue
1960	W.E. Black	North Olive Avenue
1960	Bert Brown	North Olive Avenue
1960-1968	W. Ray Duncan	North Olive Avenue 36th Street
1966-1967	Wayne Speer	36th Street
1968-1982	Bill Hatcher	36th Street
1972-1973	Larry Grizzell	36th Street
1974-1998	Dean Reynolds	36th Street
1974-1980	Kerry Cain	36th Street
1980-1981	Gary McMahan	36th Street
1980-1982	Glann Lee	36th Street
1982-Present	*Dan Jenkins	36th Street 4067 Leo Lane
1984	Steve Ellis	36th Street

— Men Who Have Served As Preachers —

Year	Name	Location
1986-1987	Bruce DeMoss	36th Street
1986-1990	Jay Winter	36th Street
1990-2008	Ron Brackett	36th Street 4067 Leo Lane
1997-Present	*David Sproule, II	36th Street 4067 Leo Lane
2004-2008 2014-Present	*Josh Blackmer	4067 Leo Lane
2006-2011	Douglas Alvarenga	4067 Leo Lane
2009-2011	Casey Haynes	4067 Leo Lane
2023-Present	*Robert J. Lupo	4067 Leo Lane

"Preach the word! Be ready in season and out of season. Convince, rebuke, exhort, with all longsuffering and teaching."
(2 Tim. 4:2)

*Currently Serving as a Preacher

— Secretaries —

Year	Name	Location
Early 1960s	Leann Flowers	North Olive Avenue
1966-1968	Ann Haines	36th Street
1968	Lee Osborne	36th Street
1969-1973	Frankie Mitchell	36th Street
1973-1975	Judy Witt	36th Street
1975-Present	*June Haines Pack	36th Street 4067 Leo Lane
1978-2005	Marian Holland	36th Street 4067 Leo Lane
2005-2007	Naomi Haltom Ingram	4067 Leo Lane
2008-2009	Amanda Rivera	4067 Leo Lane
2008-2010	Lindsey Jenkins McPherson	4067 Leo Lane
2010-Present	*Cindy Nelson	4067 Leo Lane

— Office Staff —

Year	Name	Location
2022-Present	*Ivan Villard, Jr. (Operations Manager)	4067 Leo Lane

"For we are God's fellow workers; you are God's field, you are God's building."
(1 Cor. 3:9)

***Currently Serving on the Office Staff*

Made in the USA
Columbia, SC
23 June 2023